MAN
as
male and female

*A Study in Sexual Relationships
from a Theological Point of View*

by PAUL K. JEWETT

*Professor of Systematic Theology,
Fuller Theological Seminary,
and
Dean of The Young Life Institute.*

William B. Eerdmans Publishing Company
Grand Rapids

I dedicate this book to my wife Christine.

Library of Congress Cataloging in Publication Data

Jewett, Paul King.
  Man as male and female.

  Bibliography: p. 189.
  1. Sex (Theology).   2. Woman (Theology) — Biblical
teaching.   I. Title.
BT708.J48   220.8'301 41'2   74-32471
ISBN 0-8028-1597-9

Reprinted, February 1990

Grateful acknowledgment is due the following for permission to use material —

Reprinted from *Die Ehe im Neuen Testament* by Heinrich Baltensweiler; and from *Der Mensch im Widerspruch* and *Dogmatik II* by Emil Brunner. By permission of Theologischer Verlag, Zürich.

Reprinted from *The Feminine Mystique* by Betty Friedan. By permission of W. W. Norton and Company, Inc. Copyright © 1963, 1974 by Betty Friedan.

Reprinted from *Die Frau in der antiken Welt und im Urchristentum* by J. Leipoldt. By permission of Gütersloher Verlagshaus Gerd Mohn, Gütersloh.

Reprinted from *Jerusalem in the Time of Jesus* by J. Jeremias, trans. by C. Cave et al., 1969. By permission of Fortress Press.

Reprinted from *The Second Sex* by Simone de Beauvoir, trans. by H. M. Parshley. By permission of Alfred A. Knopf, Inc. Copyright 1953.

Reprinted from *Sexual Relation in Christian Thought*, 1959, by D. S. Bailey; and from *Was Jesus Married?*, 1970, by Wm. E. Phipps. By permission of Harper and Row, Publishers, Inc.

Reprinted from the *Summa Theologica* by St. Thomas Aquinas, trans. by the Fathers of the English Dominican Province, 1948. By permission of Benziger Bruce and Glencoe, Inc.

Reprinted from the *Theological Dictionary of the New Testament*, ed. by Gerhard Kittel and Gerhard Friedrich, and trans. by Geoffrey Bromiley. By permission of the Wm. B. Eerdmans Publishing Company.

Contents

Foreword

It is typical of the author of this volume, Professor Paul Jewett, that, having written a book about male/female partnership in the image of God, he should ask a woman to write the Foreword. Typical, because his erudition is not a product of the ivory tower but arises out of real experience and holds enormous implications for real experience. Were the thesis of this book to find widespread acceptance, such acceptance would imply great changes in the church and in the quality of individual Christian living. Although it is almost unheard-of to ask a woman to write the Foreword to a theological treatise, for fear of rendering suspect the seriousness and profundity of the work, the author shows himself a follower, in this regard, of One who often took such risks, speaking to despised women in public, sometimes picturing God in female terms, and making women the first witnesses of his resurrection.

I hope I will not be thought sacrilegious if I say that writing the Foreword to this book makes me feel like those first witnesses to the risen Christ. I do not make the comparison lightly. Having been brought up in an environment which never failed to impress upon me my second-class citizenship in the family of God, having been taught that my training in literary exegesis was useless to the church because women must keep silent there, I feel in the presence of this study what many first-century women must have felt as they listened to the Master. By sticking closely to the text of Scripture, Professor Jewett demonstrates beyond the shadow of a doubt that Jesus' behavior toward women was revolutionary, that he deliberately and radically broke with the patriarchal and male supremacist attitudes of

7

Hebrew culture, "restoring to the woman the full humanity which was given her by the Creator when he made Man male and female." And he does so in a completely direct fashion, without a trace of the condescension so common to discussions of "the woman question" or the "problem of woman's role and status."

Professor Jewett recognizes that such formulations are presumptuous and arrogant, since they presuppose that "man's place in life has been determined and is beyond dispute." Instead he searches the Scriptures concerning the "man/woman question," the question of the right relationship between the two, "a question that can never be resolved so long as one member presupposes that his role in the relationship is self-evident." The impact of the author's tone will probably be lost on male readers, who have never known how bewildered and dehumanized it makes one feel to be the neglected sex during a lesson on God's giving gifts to men. But it is no mystery to me that first-century women were transformed by their contact with Jesus and even risked their lives to stand by him at his crucifixion; for this rabbi, unlike any other they had met, assumed their personhood and treated them with the same respect he accorded to male persons. The experience of reading Dr. Jewett's scholarly and searching study of the man/woman relationship has been for me, as it were, an epiphany, a manifestation of our Lord's own spirit. Hence my feeling of humility and sincere gratitude for what he has sought to do.

Ultimately, however, a biblical thesis is established not through feelings (no matter how exalted), but through obedience to the laws of disciplined reason in handling the evidence of the text. The author is too consistent to argue that although woman is equal to man, she must nevertheless obey him as her superior in the social hierarchy. To my knowledge, he is the first evangelical theologian to face squarely the fact that if woman must of necessity be subordinate, she must of necessity be inferior. I have shown elsewhere how valiantly the seventeenth-century poet John Milton wrestled with this issue, picturing woman as nobly as possible within the concept of the Great Chain of Being, yet unavoidably committed to the inferiority of prelapsarian woman because of his commitment to the hierarchical concept of the universe.[1]

Many modern theologians, ashamed to proclaim female inferiority because of all sorts of evidence to the contrary, yet assuming that the Bible forces them to such a position, have tried to have it both ways. But because of an unthreatened faith and an unthreatened masculinity, Professor Jewett is free to re-examine biblical evidence from the ground up, finding that "the argument for female subordination is incompatible with (a) the biblical narratives of Man's creation, (b) the revelation which is given us in the life of Jesus, and (c) Paul's fundamental statement of Christian liberty in the epistle to the Galatians." Like a good scholar, he does not flinch from minute and dispassionate examination of the most difficult passages, including the apparent discrepancies in the Genesis creation narratives and in the attitudes of the Apostle Paul.[2]

Dr. Jewett is not the first person to argue that "a theology of Man that is male-oriented is surely not one that is based on revelation" and that "it is high time the church should press on to the full implementation of the apostle's vision concerning the equality of the sexes in Christ." But to my knowledge he is the first male evangelical theologian to argue this point on the basis of patient, thorough, and profound explication of all the Scriptures applicable to the relationship between male and female in society and the church.

And he does not try to hide behind the excuse that sexual egalitarianism would destroy all hierarchy in society, so that there would no longer be any levels of authority, only a miserable anarchy. That type of argument from extremes has been used long enough as a way of evading the responsibility of being just and fair to 51 per cent of the human race. Professor Jewett rightly comments that "To perceive the personal dimension as an I/Thou fellowship does not imply an egalitarianism that knows no . . . super- and subordination in society." Instead he points out that both men and women were born "in some cir-

1. "Milton and Women's Liberation," Milton Quarterly, VII (December, 1973).

2. See my articles concerning Women's Liberation and the Bible in The Texas Quarterly, XVI (Autumn, 1973) and in The Christian Herald, 95 (December, 1972).

cumstances to command, in others to obey." And the more personal the relationship between men and women (as in marriage), the *less* commanding and obeying there needs to be.

Man as Male and Female is not an easy book, nor is it a book to be sampled at random or quarried in segments by busy students who want a quick addition to their bibliography. The steady logic of its argument, the sane balance of its tone, can be experienced only by a thorough reading from beginning to end. Every detail, including the lengthy critique of Karl Barth, is vital to the biblical case which Professor Jewett patiently and truthfully builds. Those who really care about human persons and really care about accurate interpretation of the Bible will be willing to work through the argument every inch of the way. They will be amply rewarded.

To anyone who has been deeply involved in the woman's liberation movement, the most troubling segment of the book will be Professor Jewett's section concerning androgyny. It is, of course, essential to an accurate interpretation of Genesis that the Platonic myth of the original androgyne and its modern applications should be refuted. Hence the author rejects Berdyaev's concept that "A man in whom the feminine principle were completely absent would be an abstract being and a woman in whom the masculine principle were completely absent would not be a personality." This rejection will trouble women's liberationists because they are actively engaged in overcoming the unjust sexual stereotypes which assign to man everything that is active, aggressive, intellectual, and dominant, while assigning to woman everything that is passive, submissive, intuitive, and dependent. In a culture full of such stereotypes, it is natural that psychologists must argue that men need that which is "feminine" and women need that which is "masculine" if either is to be a complete person. The best of these psychologists are not arguing for "unisex," nor are they in any way trying to obliterate genuine sexual distinctions. They are combating the stereotypes which impose upon both men and women impossibly fragmented concepts of what it means to be either.

Professor Jewett, however, is not thinking about stereotypes. His concern is rather the abiding reality of the creative act by which Man was made male and female, so that each sex realizes itself only in proper relationship with the other (a total relating which goes far beyond the individual relationship of marriage, as he is quick to point out). Within their own context the psychologists are right to insist that as long as intellect, aggression, and the like are stereotyped as masculine and intuition, submissiveness, and the like are stereotyped as feminine, the healthy person will need to embrace both "masculine" and "feminine" elements; but at the same time within his own context the author is equally right to reject the androgynous ideal of "transcending sexuality" in terms of a humanity that would overcome all sexual differences. Both the psychologists and the author are arguing in their own context for the acceptance of reality. Men are not exclusively creatures of aggression nor are women exclusively dependent; and these realities must be accepted rather than warped and distorted by the imposition of society's expectations. Yet God created Man male and female, and any attempt to deny this reality leads to disorders both in the individual personality and in society as a whole. The apparent disagreement between Professor Jewett and those psychologists who argue that each individual is psychically bisexual is therefore more apparent than real. He is thinking in terms of the deepest realities of creation, while the psychologists are thinking in terms of overcoming the psychic damage of society's ironclad stereotypes.

Crucial to the author's entire argument is the point that Christians today should not strive to maintain the status quo reflected in the first-century church as though that example were meant to establish the norm for all times and all places. Rather, Christians today should seek to implement the liberating principles of the New Testament in order to achieve the New Testament ideal of a redeemed humanity in Christ. To be consistent, any church which insists on keeping women in a first-century relationship to men must also insist upon the reinstitution of slavery as it existed in the first century. New Testament remarks to slaves were intended to comfort and instruct them in a situation which could not be changed overnight, while New Testament principles of Christian brotherhood were intended ultimately to destroy slavery. Similarly, New Testament remarks about female subordination were intended to comfort and instruct women in a situation which could not be changed overnight, while New Testament principles of love and mutual respect were intended ultimately to destroy all subordination of one half of the human race to the other. Any church or individual who can make cultural distinctions in connection with slavery must in all honesty make similar distinctions about the relationship between men and women as pictured in the New Testament. The liberating vision of Galatians 3:28, not the stultifying first-century actuality, is the ideal to implement.

Recently, in discussion with a Christian preacher who is sure that the New Testament teaches the everlasting subordination of women, I asked the meaning of Paul's remark that in Christ there is neither male nor female. The preacher responded, "I have no idea what he meant — I only know he said that women must be quiet in church and must obey their husbands." The preacher's tone left no reasonable doubt that not only did he not *know* what Paul meant, he did not *care*. Yet this same preacher often insists that it is the responsibility of the church to declare "*all* the counsel of God" (Acts 20:27). *Man as Male and Female* is a book for those who are unwilling to leave in limbo certain passages which threaten to destroy their preconceptions. In other words, *Man as Male and Female* is addressed to those persons who really *do* care about declaring and practicing "all the counsel of God." They that have ears to hear, let them hear.

Virginia Ramey Mollenkott, Ph.D.
Chairman, Department of English
William Paterson College of New Jersey
Wayne, New Jersey

Abstract of the Argument

A voluminous literature has appeared on the so-called "woman question." While much of this effort reflects a Christian point of view and all of it bears on issues vital to human life, relatively little has been written from the perspective of Christian dogmatics as such. And what has been written is, too often, but a reaffirmation (*sans* its less palatable features) of the traditional approach. Moreover, what is genuinely new is sometimes lost in the larger discussions to which dogmatic theology is given. In this study, I have sought to gather together in a single essay what has been said by the theologians about Man as male and female, both that which reflects the traditional view and that which seeks to go beyond it.[1]

In doing so, I take the position that the "woman question" is a "man/woman" question which has its roots, theologically speaking, in the doctrine of the *imago Dei*. While I do not reject the classical view of the image as having to do with Man's unique powers of self-transcendence by which he exercises dominion over creation as God's vicegerent, I do insist that Man's creation in the divine image is so related to his creation as male and female that the latter may be looked upon as an exposition of the former. His sexuality is not simply a mechanism for procreation which Man has in common with the animal world; it is rather a part of what it means to be like the Creator. As God is a fellowship in himself (Trinity) so Man is a fellowship in himself, and the fundamental form of this fellow-

---

1. Throughout the course of the discussion, as in this summary of it, I seek to relieve the semantic problem by capitalizing the word "man" when used generically, while leaving it in the lower case when it designates the male of the species in distinction to the female.

13

ship, so far as Man is concerned, is that of male and female. This view of Man's being, I argue, implies a partnership in life; and the proper understanding of the account of woman's creation from and for the man is in every way compatible with such a theology of sexual partnership.

The major portion of the study is devoted to the question of a hierarchical view of the man/woman relationship. My own conclusion is that the case for hierarchy, in the last analysis, requires one to argue not only for the priority but also the superiority of the male. The classical statement of the argument plainly affirms as much: the woman is subordinate to the man because she is inferior to him. The contemporary statement, by repudiating the notion of the woman's inferiority, has involved itself in an antinomy. The entire case for sexual hierarchy becomes a *non sequitur* which may be summarized as follows: (a) the woman is in no way inferior to the man, (b) yet she is different from him, (c) therefore she is subordinate to him. This argument is not compelling. The difference between the sexes does not entail a relationship of super- and subordination.

I therefore reject a hierarchical model of the man/woman relationship in favor of a model of partnership. According to the creation ordinance, man and woman are properly related when they accept each other as equals whose difference is mutually complementary in all spheres of life and human endeavor. In arriving at this conclusion I place great weight upon the exegetical possibilities of the Genesis account of human origins and especially upon the way in which Jesus related to women. The contrast between the data of Scripture, in this regard, and the view of woman stemming from the patriarchal culture of Old Testament Israel is carefully reviewed, as both these strands of redemptive history meet in the apostle Paul, the supreme interpreter of the revelation of God in Christ. The question of Paul the former rabbi versus Paul the apostle of Christ is explored with the help of the distinction between his perception of the truth and his implementation of it in the Greco-Roman world of the first century, the world in which the Christian church was born. Appealing to the issue of slavery as illustrative of this distinction, I make the plea that the church today should canonize, not the implementation, but the insight of the apostle into the manner in which the man/woman relationship is redeemed in Christ.

To the main argument I have attached divers addenda of varying lengths, treating of such questions as sex in the final eschaton, whether Jesus was married, "female" uncleanness, misogyny in Western thought, and the ordination of women to the Christian ministry. The entire discussion concludes with an epilogue on the ontology of sex with special attention to the "Eternal Feminine," a concept which I reject as an instance of the larger error of understanding the woman in terms of the man rather than understanding both in terms of their mutual relationship to each other and to God.

MAN
as
male and female

I

Introduction

In seeking an answer to the question, "What is Man?"
thinkers in all ages have sensed the unique importance of the
quest, for in the study of Man, Man is the object of his own
inquiry, the knower is the known. And this quest, understandably, has turned on the issue of subject and object: Is the clue
to the mystery of Man that he is a subject, i.e. a free, transcendent spirit; or is he an object, a body in time and space,
whose life in the last analysis is but a fortuitous collocation of
atoms, a complex instance of the fundamental laws of physics?
So engrossed have thinkers been in adjudicating this question,
so anxious have they been to know whether Man, if not a little
lower than the angels, is at least a little higher than the animals,
that they have given surprisingly scant attention to the fact that
Man is *male and female*.

In this regard the theologians have largely followed the
example of the philosophers. Though Scripture plainly affirms:
"And God created Man in his own image, in the image of
God created he him; *male and female* created he them" (Gen.
1:27), the teachers of the church have seen significance only in
the fact that Man is in the divine image and have rather ig-
nored the further fact that he is male and female. Without
question the affirmation of this text that Man is uniquely
endowed with the divine image is fundamental to a Christian
view of Man; but it is striking that the theologians should have
bestowed so much indifference upon the affirmation that is
immediately subjoined, which tells us that this uniquely endowed creature is male and female.

This neglected feature of the biblical doctrine of Man is

elaborated in the familiar creation narrative found in Genesis 2:18-25, where it is expressly stated that God made woman and brought her to the man because it was not good that man should be alone. If this is so, surely it is not good that one should develop a doctrine of Man in terms of the male alone. If Man is male and female by the Creator's decision and act, so that *her* creation is in some sense the completion of *his* creation, then a theology of Man that is male-oriented is surely not one that is based on revelation, one that strives to think God's thoughts after him. As a corrective to this imbalance, the following statement has been prepared on the subject: Man as male and female.

Since Genesis 1:27 brings the question of Man as male and female into the closest possible conjunction with Man's creation in the divine image, we shall begin our discussion by asking how human sexuality is related to the *imago Dei*. It is the doctrine of the *imago* which distinguishes the biblical view of Man from all other anthropologies, whether they be ancient or modern, philosophical or scientific; and therefore it is proper that a doctrine of Man as man and woman should begin at this point. From this starting point we shall go on to explore the fundamental question of how man and woman ought to be related in the larger partnership of life with its manifold and creative possibilities.

Theologians have traditionally sought the answer to this question in the institution of marriage. The intimate personal relationship of a man and a woman as husband and wife has served as the principal paradigm for understanding how men and women should be related in all of life. As the individual man is the head of his family, so man generally, not woman, is the head of the human family. His is the prerogative and responsibility of leadership in human affairs. This is true not only in the church (the fellowship of faith working by love) but to a lesser degree in the school (the fellowship of learning), economic enterprise (the fellowship of service), and even the state (the fellowship of justice).

In this study, however, we shall not follow this traditional approach. Rather we shall view the form of sexual polarity in which God has given us our humanity as the fundamental creation ordinance, from which perspective we shall seek to under-

stand the man/woman relationship in all the concrete structures of life, including marriage. In other words, we shall
endeavor to answer the question: What is the Christian understanding of Man as male and female? Having answered that
question, we shall then ask: How does this understanding illumine the relationship of man and woman, not only in marriage,
but in life as a whole? Of course our conclusions as to how man
and woman are to be related in life generally will have decided
implications for marriage, that most intimate of all relationships, as well as for the other structures of fellowship by which
our life is made human. But we shall touch upon these implications only incidentally, since our purpose is not to answer
specific questions about marriage and the family, women in
the Christian ministry, and the like. Rather we shall deal with
the fundamental question: How ought we as Christians to
understand the man/woman relationship as such? For it is
as such, as man *or* woman, man *and* woman, that we share
life together.

Because the doctrine of the divine image is fundamental
to the ensuing discussion, it will, perhaps, enhance the clarity
of the argument if we simply state at this time our commitment
to the following assumptions concerning the nature of Man:

Man is created in the image of God. We do not understand the word "image" to mean an exact "replica" or "dupli-
cate" but rather a "correspondence" or "reflection."[1] Man may
be said uniquely to reflect God at the creaturely level in that he
alone, being endowed by his Maker with the powers of rational
transcendence and self-determining will, is related to God and
his neighbor as a free and responsible subject. This is not to
denigrate the body as of no significance in the Christian view
of Man. But the fundamental stress in the Old Testament upon
the divine transcendence (note the Old Testament prohibition
against making graven images) and in the New Testament upon
conformity to the image of Christ, set forth primarily in terms
of ethical and religious qualities (Rom. 8:29; Col. 3:10), tends

---

1. Though "image" (צלם) and "likeness" (דמות) in Gen. 1:26 are
essentially parallel, the movement from one to the other probably reflects
the author's desire for explanatory qualification. Hence our preference for
"correspondence" or "reflection" over "replica."

to put the weight of emphasis for dogmatics on Man as subject rather than object.[2]

Man is a sinner, fallen short of the glory of God. Man may be said to be fallen in that he uses the powers with which he is uniquely endowed by his Maker in an effort to achieve a proud autonomy. In this perversion of his true self, he revolts against God and exploits his neighbor, thereby destroying his freedom and living as though he were not a responsible subject. The tyranny of the man over the woman (Gen. 3:16, in the context of the curse) is a notable example of such a perversion of his humanity.

Man, as the recipient of divine grace in Christ, is redeemed. Man may be said to be redeemed in that he is being enabled more and more to live a life of responsibility in love toward God and his neighbor and so is renewed in the divine image. As redeemed, Man strives to use the powers with which he is uniquely endowed by his Maker to realize a life of fellowship wherein God is supreme and his neighbor a subject like himself. Inasmuch as the Christian church is the sphere in which such redeeming grace is principally operative, the place of woman and her rights must be a prime concern of the theologians as teachers in the church.

2. Cf. Walther Eichrodt, *Theology of the Old Testament,* II (Philadelphia: Westminster, 1961).

II

The Theological Options

A. A Summary Statement

There are, broadly speaking, three schools of thought about the sexual polarity of man's existence, which are reflected, at least to some degree, in representative Christian writers. Rarely, of course, do the affirmations of any major thinker fall neatly into one of these perspectives. But in stating them, one can see what the options are and also recognize where the influential dogmaticians have severally taken their stand.

First of all, there is the position that the male/female distinction has nothing to contribute to our understanding of Man as created in the divine image. In fact, to consider this aspect of Man's being in an effort to define his essential nature would only confuse the issue and lead us astray in our thinking. True humanity transcends sexuality. We must, then, think in terms of oneness, not diversity, in terms of unity, not polarity, if we would think rightly about Man.

A second view affirms that while the male/female distinction is not an essential part of the doctrine of Man, it is evident from Scripture that both the male and the female share alike the distinctive endowments whereby Man differs from the animals; that is to say, men and women both participate in the divine image. Therefore, in understanding Man, there should be no striving to transcend the distinction between male and female, nor appeal made to the masculine principle, in contrast to the feminine, as the primary and proper paradigm of humanity. Emphasis in modern theology on the dynamic understanding of Man as man-in-fellowship has given a fillip to this traditional view.

According to a third view, to be in the image of God *is* to be male and female. Not only do men and women alike partici-pate in the divine image, but their fellowship as male and female is what it *means* to be in the image of God. One should not then subsume the question of Man's sexual duality under the rubric of marriage and the family, as has been done in the traditional view just mentioned. While marriage is perhaps the most intimate form of human fellowship, it is not the most basic. Men and women may *become* related as husband and wife, and many do; but they *are* related as men and women by virtue of God's creative act. To be Man is to be male *or* female, male *and* female, and consequently the discussion of this mysterious duality cannot be postponed until one has said what is to be said about Man as such. To talk about Man as such is precisely to talk about Man as man and woman.

We shall now look more closely at these three approaches in the order in which they have been mentioned, giving special attention to the last with its emphasis on the male/female structure of Man's existence as the meaning of the *imago Dei*.

B. *The Androgynous Ideal*

According to the first position mentioned, to probe the meaning of the male/female dualism of human existence is, in a way, to embarrass rather than illumine the human quest for self-understanding. This position has enjoyed only a quali-fied acceptance in the ongoing theological discussion, since it is obviously difficult to harmonize with biblical revelation. Influenced by Plato's report (*Symposium*) of primeval androg-ynous beings, Philo of Alexandria first sought to understand Genesis 1:26, "Let us make Man," as a reference to the "Idea," *Man*. This *Man*, the *Idea* to which the thought in the mind corresponds, is in the divine image — incorporeal, immortal, neither male nor female. By contrast, empirical Man (Gen. 2) is body and soul, male and female, and mortal. Later rabbinic exegesis echoes this androgynous understanding of the first creation narrative.[1]

1. Cf. J. Leipoldt, *Die Frau in der antiken Welt und im Urchristentum* (Gütersloher Verlagshaus [Gerd Mohn], 1962), pp. 116-117.

This effort to harmonize the first creation narrative with the ancient Greek myth of the androgyne or hermaphrodite cannot be sustained.[2] Though the subject is Man in the divine image, Genesis 1:26 goes on to speak of *them*, not *him*, as having dominion over all the earth. And the reason for the plural is made plain in the next verse, which says, "Male and female created he *them*" (v. 27). Hence there is no justification for emending the text to read in the singular (אתם to אתו). Furthermore, the terms in the phrase "male and female" (זכר ונקבה) are nominal, not adjectival; they denote the male and the female of the species respectively in their concrete, individual manifestation. To the same effect is the statement in Genesis 5:2: "Male and female he created them, and he blessed them and named them Man when they were created." Commenting on these words, Rabbi Simeon, as recorded in the *Zohar*, states explicitly:

> God does not make his abode in any place where male and female are not found together; nor are blessings found save in such a place, as it is written: "And he blessed them and called their name Man on the day that they were created." Note that it says *them* and *their* name, not *him* and *his* name. The male is not even called man until he is united with the female.[3]

Yet for all the clarity of the Hebrew text, there have been those in the Christian tradition who have found it difficult to understand original Man in terms of the distinction between male and female. Especially in Eastern Christianity there has been a tendency, going back to some of the early Fathers, to relate Man's sexual polarity to his fallen condition rather than to his original condition. The Greek Fathers came to this position not from their view of Man but from their view of sin as basically sensuality, of which sexual lust was the principal example.

2. In Greek mythology Hermaphroditus, son of Hermes and Aphrodite, was joined in one body with the nymph Salmacis. He (?) was worshipped as a divinity embodying both the male and the female principle. In modern biological science the term "hermaphrodite" is used to designate organisms that are bisexual, a phenomenon that is uncommon in the more complex orders of living beings. Such androgynous organisms are frequent, however, in certain forms of marine life, some being both male and female at once, others beginning adult life as males and then turning into females.

3. As quoted in D. S. Bailey, *Sexual Relation in Christian Thought* (New York: Harper, 1959), p. 272.

(The Augustinian view of sin as basically pride, by contrast, dominated the Latin church.) Origen, the greatest of the early Greek theologians, not only regarded all sex activity as sinful but actually mutilated himself to avoid the passion.[4]

Among contemporary theologians the mystic Nicholas Berdyaev of the Russian Orthodox Church is, perhaps, the major spokesman for the view that man's sexual duality is an expression of his fallen nature. According to Berdyaev, Man is really a bisexual being combining both the masculine and feminine principle in different proportions. A man in whom the feminine principle were completely absent would be an abstract being, and a woman in whom the masculine principle were completely absent would not be a personality. The masculine principle is essentially personal and anthropological, while the feminine principle is essentially communal and cosmic. It is only in the union of these two principles that we have complete humanity. This union is realized in every man and woman within their androgynous natures, but in the fallen world the two principles not only seek union but also wage war against each other. According to Berdyaev, the Oedipus complex, to which Freud and the psychoanalysts attach universal meaning, may be interpreted symbolically and mystically in the light of this cosmic struggle between the sexes. The masculine and the feminine principles, fatherhood and motherhood, are struggling for predominance. Hence Man cannot live in peace and harmony while he remains a sexual being.

The great anthropological myth, which alone can be the basis of an anthropological metaphysic, says Berdyaev, is the myth of the androgyne, first told in Plato's *Symposium* and later occupying a central place in the Gnosticism of Böhme. As a sexual, halved, divided being, Man is doomed to disharmony, to passionate longing and dissatisfaction. Original sin is connected, in the first instance, with division into two sexes and the fall of the androgyne, that is, of Man as a complete being. It involves the loss of human virginity and the formation of the bad masculine and the bad feminine. This leads to incalculable consequences for the fate of the world and for Man's moral life. Though Christian asceticism has made heroic efforts to

4. See Reinhold Niebuhr, *The Nature and Destiny of Man*, I (New York: Charles Scribner's Sons, 1941), p. 228.

overcome the horror and the curse of sex and can claim great achievements, yet the problem has never been completely solved.

Sex is the source of life and of death. Sex, which has cleft in two the androgynous image of Man, dooms Man to death, to the bad infinity of lives and deaths. Erotic love always brings death with it. This is brought out with the force of genius in Wagner's *Tristan and Isolde*. The great poets and artists have seen this connection between love and death. Man is a sick, wounded, and disharmonious creature, in the thinking of Berdyaev, primarily because he is sexual, that is, a bisected being who has lost his wholeness and original integrity.[5]

A much more persistent and subtle challenge to the Christian doctrine of Man as essentially a duality of male and female comes from Greek philosophy, especially the tradition of Idealism. From Plato to Hegel the thinking self has been viewed as the true locus of knowledge and reality. The subject of the sentence with which Descartes began his philosophy, *Cogito ergo sum* (I think, therefore I am), is not an "I" in relationship to a "thou," but an independent subject who understands himself in terms of himself.

Contemporary theologians have been severely critical of this idealistic approach, as every student of theology knows. How often it has been affirmed that such an understanding of the self is really a misunderstanding which leads to the transcendental Self of the ethicist, the autonomous, absolute Self of the metaphysician, the Self that knows no authority outside itself and so confuses itself with the divine Self in a pantheistic denial of the Christian doctrine of "the absolute qualitative difference" between the creature and the Creator. The antidote (it is affirmed) to this abstract philosophic monism, this "static" conception of Man, is the view that Man is Man only in fellowship, fellowship with God and with his neighbor; there can be no "I" without a "thou."

Such a "dynamic" view of Man seems, indeed, to reflect a genuine biblical emphasis. Scripture always understands Man in terms of his relationship to God (whether negatively related to him in sin or positively in grace). And more especially,

5. See Nicholas Berdyaev, *The Destiny of Man*, ch. III, section 3, "Sex: The Masculine and the Feminine" (London: Geoffrey Bles, 1954).

Scripture expressly declares that it is not good that man should be alone (Gen. 2:18), for which reason he is given the woman, that as partners together they may share and fulfill a common destiny in life. The church, then, in framing its doctrine of Man, must resist the temptation to minimize the primeval fellowship of the creation ordinance whereby Man is male and female. As Barth has warned, to neutralize the sexes is to dehumanize Man.[6]

In fact, precisely in their relationship to God, which is the one thing they have in common, the man and the woman cannot cease to be what they are: man or woman, man and woman. There is no room, then, for the thought that it would be beautiful and glorious for human existence — so satisfying and purifying in this whole sordid realm — if the man and the woman somehow could transcend their sex in terms of a humanity embracing both in a higher unity, a unity that would overcome all differences. To think this way would be to suppose that Man knows better than God the Creator who, in this regard, has made his will simple and clear. In brief, for mankind all is in order so long, and only so long, as the man and the woman, whether in a single state or within the marriage bond, will to be human beings ever fully conscious of their sex — and not only conscious of it but also honestly happy in it, each thankful to God that he or she can be a human being of a particular sex, proceeding on his or her own unique way through life with a sober and good conscience.[7]

6. See Karl Barth, *Kirchliche Dogmatik*, III/4, pp. 173f., hereafter cited as *K.D.* (Zollikon-Zurich: Evangelischer Verlag, 1951). In the English translation, *Church Dogmatics*, III/4, tr. A. T. Mackay, T. H. L. Parker, Harold Knight, Henry A. Kennedy, and John Marks (Edinburgh: Clark, 1961), see pp. 156f. References to English translations of German works cited will hereafter be given within square brackets in the notes.

7. See Barth, *K.D.*, III/4, pp. 173-174 [156-157]. As an example of the error which he here rejects, Barth cites Simone de Beauvoir's celebrated remarks: "*On ne naît pas femme, on le devient*" ("One is not born a woman, one becomes a woman"), *Le Deuxieme Sex*, II, p. 13. But it is doubtful that he read her correctly. She does not mean to say that sexuality is an accidental circumstance of humanity in contrast to the boundary situations of birth and death. Rather she is affirming that modern woman has been made what she is by the machinations of Western androcentric culture. Hence the struggle to which she calls the woman to be truly human (*l'être humain*) is a struggle for her birth right as a member of the human race. One can reject Mlle de Beauvoir's fundamentally anti-Christian Existentialism and still hear the truth she has spoken in this word.

C. The Traditional View Which
Subsumes Human Sexuality Under Marriage

Although the view that stresses unity, seeking to understand Man as an androgynous Subject transcending the duality
of male and female (position one), has been generally rejected
in Christian theology, it has seldom occurred to the theologians
even to mention the fellowship of the sexes when discoursing
on the nature of Man in the image of God. It is generally assumed, to be sure, that sexuality is a creation of God, so that
both man and woman are in the divine image (position two).
But in the traditional discussion of what it means to say that
Man is like God, there is only passing allusion to the fact that
Man is like God as Man-in-fellowship, that is, as male and
female.

Augustine, for example, even when referring to Man as
the image of the Trinity, did not think in terms of the fellowship of man and woman; in fact, he did not think of fellowship
at all. Man is like the Trinity in that he (1) is, (2) knows that
he is, and (3) delights in his being and in the knowledge of
this being.[8] In St. Thomas, none of the nine articles in the
Summa which treat of the creation of Man in the divine image
touches upon the male/female relationship.[9] Likewise with Calvin. In the *Institutes*, I, xv, he discourses at length on human
nature as created by God: Man is a diversity of soul and body,
a being endowed with free will, and so forth. But he never
says a word about woman until II, viii, 43, where, in expounding the seventh commandment, he observes that celibacy is the
gift of the few and marriage the guarantor of chastity in the
many. In all this, he simply assumes what had not been ques-
tioned for centuries, that is, that the woman was given to the
man as a helper in the one and only work in which he really
needed her help, namely, the work of procreation. It was
deemed obvious that the fellowship of the sexes has to do with
the command to be fruitful, to multiply, and to replenish the
earth (Gen. 1:28). The fellowship of man and woman is con-
summated in marriage and in the family that issues from this

8. Augustine, *De civitate Dei*, XI, p. 26.
9. *Summa Theologica*, Q. XCIII; "The Production of the Woman" (Q.
XCII) is treated as a separate subject distinct from that of the creation
of man.

conjugal union. In other words, though the male/female differentiation is associated in Scripture with creation in the divine
image (Gen. 1:27), in the discussion of the theologians it is
almost exclusively associated with the command to procreate
(Gen. 1:28).

Some theologians have more recently affirmed that Man
is Man in virtue of his fellowship with God and his neighbor.
Yet even they have not pressed this dynamic aspect of the
image to mean the fellowship of male and female *as such*.
Though the words of Scripture, "It is not good that man should
be alone," are emphasized, it is more or less assumed that the
divine solution was the creation of another human being like
the man in distinction to the animals. That this other human
being who stood over against the man as his "thou" was not
only *like* the man but also *different* from him, in that *she* was
a *woman*, is seldom mentioned, save to refute the suggestion
that it ought to be. Berkouwer, for example, while admitting
that the affirmation "God created Man in his own image" is
immediately followed by "male and female created he them,"
insists that this does not necessarily mean that the second
clause defines the first. There is no implication that the image
of God lies in the relationship between man and woman.[10]

Even the current surge of interest in sex, marriage, and the
emancipation of women has not substantially altered the thinking of theologians. They still stand, for the most part, on the
middle ground where they have traditionally stood. According
to this *via media*, the biblical account of Man's creation says
no more — and no less — than that human beings, both male
and female, are in God's image. Men and women are in the
divine image as men and as women, but the male/female distinction and the relationship that it creates are not, as such,
that wherein the image consists.

Emil Brunner, who employed the personalism of Ebner
and Buber more creatively, perhaps, than any other theologian
of his day, anticipates in his doctrine of man the position that
the fellowship of the sexes belongs to the meaning of human
existence in the divine image. Yet even he does not take this
position fully, but rather reflects the traditional view. He treats

10. Cf. G. C. Berkouwer, *Man: The Image of God* (Grand Rapids: Eerdmans, 1962), p. 73.

the question of Man in the divine image (the being who is an "I from and in the Divine Thou") as distinct from the question of Man as male and female.[11]

To be sure, in separating the male/female question from that of the image, Brunner does not simply subsume it under the institution of marriage as has been traditionally done. Not marriage but sexuality is the touchstone, the definitive question in a Christian anthropology.[12] Yet, as his discussion of man and woman unfolds, the terms become more or less synonymous with husband and wife, as can be seen in the following quotation.

> The depth of this division [between man and woman] shows how deeply sexuality has been implanted in the nature of man by the Creator. Man is not a sexual being in addition to that which he is otherwise but the sex difference penetrates and determines the whole of human existence. . . . The woman, through her natural calling as wife and mother, carries a far heavier burden than the man does, as husband and father. The growth of the new human being forms part of the life of the woman far more than it forms part of the life of the man. . . . By this natural determination the woman is far more closely connected with the natural process of life, impregnated with it, restricted, but also preserved by it. Far less than her husband can she order her own life as she would like; but this is not her husband's doing; it is simply due to the fact of her motherhood. This difference penetrates into the very depths of her nature.[13]

In this quotation, the question, "What is the Christian understanding of Man as male and female?" merges with the question, "What is the Christian understanding of the roles which the male and the female, respectively, have to fulfill in the ordinance of marriage?" Such a procedure makes it obvious that Brunner does not have a theology of sexuality which would make the man/woman distinction essential to humanity. Faced with the question, "Why did God create Man male and female? What is the meaning of this duality?" his answer

11. Cf. Emil Brunner, *Der Mensch im Widerspruch* (Zurich: Zwingli Verlag, 1937) [*Man in Revolt,* tr. Olive Wyon (New York: Scribner, 1939)], where he discusses the divine image in ch. V, "The Origin: the *imago Dei,*" reserving the subject "Man and Woman" for ch. XV, many pages later.

12. Brunner, *Der Mensch im Widerspruch,* p. 340 [*Man in Revolt,* p. 345].

13. Brunner, *Der Mensch im Widerspruch,* pp. 347-348 [*Man in Revolt,* pp. 352-353].

would neither reduce the duality to mere nature, a necessary mechanism for procreation, nor exalt it to the very essence of Man's being as one who is in the image and likeness of God.

The relation between the sexes, he says, is only a penultimate, not an ultimate matter. God could have used some other mechanism than sexual pairing for propagating the race, as in fact he did in the lower orders of creation. Therefore we should not reduce the meaning of Man's male/female polarity simply to the need for propagating the race in sexual congress. Yet, on the other hand, neither should we exalt it as a permanent feature of humanity as such. The ultimate fulfillment of Man's life in the world to come, when we shall be truly like God and enjoy him forever, is a fulfillment in which sexual differentiation will have no function and hence no existence. As Jesus said: "At the resurrection of the dead they neither marry nor are given in marriage, but are like the angels in heaven" (Mk. 12:25).

The dualism of male and female, then, is the will of the Creator for Man *in this world*, as an appropriate expression of Man's creaturely dependence. Man, as finite, is so created as to be dependent upon his neighbor, unable to exist in and of himself as an autonomous and self-sufficient being. Precisely in that function in which he shares uniquely in the creative work of bringing new life into the world, Man experiences the fact of this mutual dependence in a unique fashion. Because it is not good that man should be alone, it *is* good that he be given his being in a way that fundamentally binds two beings to one another and thus makes each dependent, the one upon the other, each needing, each supplementing, the other. Thus Man has a reminder, in the very form of his humanity as male and female, that the true purpose of his life is community with God and his neighbor, and that his would-be self-sufficiency is the ultimate folly, a manifestation of pride, the root of all sin.[14]

> Sexual polarity, as such, is not itself the "I" and "thou." It is only a picture of the purpose of creation, and the natural basis of the true "I" and "thou." Sexual polarity is therefore not intended for eternity whereas the "I" and "thou," the communion and the fellowship of the Kingdom of God, is certainly intended for eternity. Hence sexual polarity is not

14. Brunner, *Der Mensch im Widerspruch*, p. 345 [*Man in Revolt*, p. 350].

itself the *imago Dei*; it is, as it were, a secondary *imago*, a reflection of the divine purpose, and, at the same time, the natural basis of true community.

Sexual love, indeed, is not itself the love at which the Creator aims, but it foreshadows true love and is also its natural presupposition. It does so in two ways: (a) the human race in its physical reality is derived from it; and (b) by it man learns what love is, as it were, in a preparatory school. Hence the sexual quality and function of man is full of the symbolism of true community. The love between the sexes, the love of man and woman, is the earthenware vessel in which true love, *agape*, is to be contained; it can therefore be thrown away when the course in the preparatory school has achieved its end.[15]

D. The View Which Grounds Human Sexuality in the Imago Dei

We turn finally (position three) to a view of Man as male and female which may be called "novel" as theological positions go, a view that understands the distinction between man and woman as itself a manifestation of the *imago Dei*. According to this view, Genesis 1:27b ("male and female made he them") is an exposition of 1:27a ("in the image of God created he him"). As with all new ideas, there is the possibility that this one will be rejected before it is clearly understood. We shall, therefore, anticipate our exposition with a few preliminary remarks.

It is commonly supposed (as we observed in the thought of Brunner) that Jesus' response to the Sadducees, "in the resurrection they neither marry nor are given in marriage, but are like the angels in heaven" (Mk. 12:15), means that all distinction between male and female will disappear in the world to come. If this is so, then one must assume that to exist as male and female is not essential to the divine image, for Man surely retains the image in the resurrection; in fact, it is only then that he is fully restored to that image.

15. Brunner, *Dogmatik*, II (Zurich: Zwingli Verlag, 1950), pp. 77-78 [*Dogmatics*, tr. Olive Wyon, II (London: Lutterworth, 1952), p. 65].

Now such a conclusion may, indeed, seem to be justified by this text, but really it is not. Exegetes have too easily inferred from Mark 12:25 that where there is no marriage there will be no male and female, because the theologians have traditionally understood the distinction between male and female in terms of marriage. There is good reason to argue, however, that it should be the other way around: marriage should be understood in terms of the male/female distinction, the latter being the more fundamental reality. If this is so, then it does not follow that a life without marriage and procreation is a life that knows no fellowship of male and female. In this regard it must be remembered that Jesus did not say that in heaven there will be no men and women, but only no marriage and giving in marriage.

Paralleling what Jesus said about marriage and the age to come are Paul's comments on the same subject in I Corinthians 7:25-35. With the passing away of this present world order, according to the apostle, marriage also shall pass away. In fact, inasmuch as the approaching new age has already broken into this present age, the apostle expected an imminent denouement. He deemed it wise, therefore, that one who was unmarried should remain so (v. 27) because the time would soon come when those who have wives would be as those who have none (v. 29).

While it may be argued that it never occurred to the apostle, with his strong Jewish antecedents, to distinguish between the fellowship of male and female in general and the institution of marriage in particular, nonetheless there is a distinction to be made, and he himself had made it in an existential, if not a theoretical, way. He had committed himself to a life of celibacy in order that he might not be burdened with the cares of this world but give himself to the things of the Lord. He resolutely chose the single life in the belief that God had called him to it, but surely he did not look upon this as a flight from his maleness. He chose to be single, but to be a man and not a woman was not his to choose. Indeed, given the circumstances and times in which he lived, he could hardly have been an apostle had he not been a man and had he not affirmed his manhood to the fullest degree in the exercise of his calling. Hence it is evident that for the apostle there was a difference between marriage and sexuality. And this difference must be kept in mind as we consider the position before us.

In elaborating the view that Man in the image of God is Man as male and female, we shall follow, in the main, the argument of Karl Barth, since he is the first major theologian to adopt such a position. This procedure will also enhance the clarity of an argument too recent to have the inner coherence of an established tradition.[16]

In common with Brunner and others who subscribe to the second position expounded above, Barth holds to a dynamic view of the *imago*: Man's being is a being-in-fellowship. All creatures created prior to Man exist, it is true, in an interrelatedness and dependency, but not in a genuine mutuality and reciprocity. In heaven and earth, land and sea, even among the living creatures, from the plants to the highest animals, there is no "thou" who is responsibly related to the divine "I." But Man exists in such a relationship from the start. And because Man is created as the one who confronts God and is confronted by God and by another like himself, he is created in the image of God. God is, in his own being, supremely free and in fellowship. Since God is no *Deus solitarius* (solitary God), but the *Deus triunus* (the triune God), i.e. God-in-relationship, there is no possibility that Man, who is in his likeness, should be *homo solitarius* (solitary Man).[17]

God gives to Man humanity, that is, freedom in fellowship; and he calls Man to prove and confirm himself in this humanity in which he has been created. God relates Man to his fellow man; he wills that Man should have his being as a being-in-encounter, in relationship, in the togetherness of "I"

16. Barth's treatment is found in K.D., III/1, § 41, pts. 2, 3, tr. J. W. Edwards, O. Bussey, and Harold Knight (1958); III/2, § 45, especially pts. 2 and 3, tr. Harold Knight, G. W. Bromiley, J. K. S. Reid, and R. H. Fuller (1960); III/4, § 54 (1961). These sections contain an abundance of materials in which Barth pursues many ancillary questions. We shall attempt to make his reasoning a little more overt by extracting, as it were, from these materials the thesis with which we are here primarily concerned. We shall also postpone a discussion of the discrepancies in his reasoning, seeming or real, until the argument has been adequately stated.

17. Barth, therefore, interprets the "Let us" of Genesis 1:26 not as a plural of majesty but, in the light of the revelation in Christ, as anticipating the Trinity. Since the text says "Let *us* make man in *our* image, after *our* likeness," which is followed by "male *and* female made he them" (v. 27), the writer must have reckoned with some kind of plurality in the Divine Being, according to Barth.

and "thou." He gives him, invites him, commands him, not only to receive his humanity as his nature but to affirm it as humanity-in-fellowship by his own decision and responsible act. God calls Man to know himself in knowing his fellow man, to enjoy himself in giving joy to his fellow man, to affirm himself in honoring his fellow man. Humanity — the unique, natural mode of being as Man — is, in its deepest root, a shared humanity (*Mitmenschlichkeit*). Humanity that is not shared humanity is *inhumanity*. And ultimately this mode of Man's being as shared humanity is what it is because Man is like God. Between God and Man there is an *analogia relationis* (an analogy of relatedness), and the univocal element in the analogy (the *tertium comparationis*) is simply Man's existence in the free differentiation and relationship of "I" and "thou."

But now comes what may be called the first great surprise in the Bible, though we seldom reflect on it due to our familiarity with the story. The Bible does not say that God "created Man in his own image, in the image of God created he him; I and thou created he them." Man is not just in fellowship with his neighbor. Rather, according to the Bible, God created Man male and female (Gen. 1:27). *The primal form of humanity, then, is the fellowship of man and woman.* How different is this from the approach of the philosophers and, to a lesser extent, of Christian theologians! While they have concerned themselves with Man's faculties of reason and moral choice, with his religious awareness of the Transcendent, the text of Genesis 1:27 makes no direct comment on Man in the image of God save to observe that he exists as male and female.[18] From a philosopher's standpoint this sexual dualism is a mere banality which (so it would seem) reminds us of Man's affinity with the animals rather than with God.

It is indeed true that Man's sexuality reflects his likeness to other creatures made by God; but, says Barth, according to the Bible there is a great deal more than the sex instinct of animals involved in the fellowship of male and female at the

---

18. The *context* of Genesis 1:27, though not the text itself, does indeed comment on Man's nature in terms of the traditional view of the *imago*. He is the creature who is given dominion (1:28), names the animals (2:19), and knows the distinction between "thou shalt" and "thou shalt not" (2:17), all of which implies rational, moral self-transcendence. Barth, of course, does not deny this.

human level. In fact (to anticipate our later discussion) to reduce Man's existence as male and female to something as purely biological as a cold sweat in propinquity is fundamentally to misunderstand Man. Man, according to the Bible, is to be understood from above downward, not from below upward. Man is the being who is uniquely related to God and thus uniquely related to his sexual partner. Only when Man has been understood theologically, according to Barth, can we understand him psychologically and biologically.

In a similar vein, Emil Brunner, reflecting on the lapidary simplicity of Genesis 1:27, comments that it seems incredibly naive to couple the statement that Man is made in the image of God with the statement that he is male and female. Yet, he affirms, ". . . on account of this one statement alone, the Bible shines out among all other books in the world as the Word of God. . . . In the whole history of man's understanding of himself, this statement has been made only once, and that is at this point."[19] The male/female distinction is far more fundamental than any individual characteristics; it "penetrates to the deepest 'metaphysical' ground of our personality and our destiny."[20]

Barth observes that we can never say "mankind" without having to say either "man" or "woman." Man has his existence in this precise difference. He exists, to be sure, in other differentiations than that of male or female. One may be gifted, or not gifted, says Barth; one must be a child, he may be a parent; one must be young, he may be old; one must be of some time, place, and race, he may be of this or that time, place or race. But in all these necessary and not-so-necessary relationships and differences, always and primarily, one is man or woman; if a spouse, either a husband or a wife; if a parent, either a father or a mother; if a child, either a son or a daughter.

Hence this difference between the man and the woman, which permeates and determines all other differences, is no mere abstraction. Humanity consists of concrete beings, of willing, thinking, feeling, speaking, acting men and women. Even in the encounter between man and another man, one remains the man who finds his true partner, his true complement, in the

19. Brunner, *Der Mensch im Widerspruch*, p. 341 [*Man in Revolt*, p. 346].
20. Brunner, *Der Mensch im Widerspruch*, p. 340 [*Man in Revolt*, p. 345].

woman; and the same is true of the encounter between woman
and woman. The male is never the male in the abstract nor
the female the female in the abstract. That is why the Scripture does not say that God created Man male *or* female —
though in a sense this is true — but male *and* female. Humanity, rightly understood, includes the "or," but it is an "or"
taken up into the "and" of the biblical ordinance of creation.

Since Barth believes that Man in this most ultimate sense
is man *and* woman, one can appreciate why he gives close attention to the second creation narrative (Gen. 2:18-25) where
the formation of woman, in distinction to man, is elaborated.
This passage, according to Barth, has one basic thrust: to fill
out the theme of Man's creation as male and female. What
was simply stated in the first creation account (Gen. 1:27)
is now enlarged upon.[21] Man is not to be a solitary creature
but one who is in partnership. ("Partner" is, says Barth, "perhaps the shortest [*kürzeste*] rendering for the term '*help corresponding to him*'" [*Hilfe, die ihm ein Gegenüber sei*].[22]) This
partner is one like himself who yet differs from him.

The animals are mentioned in the second creation narrative as a backdrop to this work of God in creating the woman.
They cannot possibly give what man must have to become truly
Man since they are not like him in any essential way. Hence
the creation of the woman as the one who alone can give man
what he must have, being essentially like him — and yet
mysteriously unlike him.

> Were this creature only *like* him, a repetition, a numerical
> multiplication, his solitariness would not be eliminated,
> for such a creature would not confront him as another
> but he would merely recognise himself in it. Again, if this
> one were only different from him, a being of a wholly
> different order, his solitariness would not be eliminated,
> for it would confront him as another, yet not as another
> which actually belongs to him . . . not as a fellow-occupant
> of this sphere fulfilling the duty allotted within it.[23]

21. Though this is the older narrative, Barth understands it to be complementary to the first narrative which contains the primary affirmation (Gen.
1:27) about Man as male and female. With this approach we concur. (See
also Gen. 5:1, 2.)
22. Barth, K.D., III/1, p. 329 [290]. Italics in German.
23. Barth, K.D., III/1, p. 331 [290].

It should also be noted that, according to Genesis 2, the relationship between the man and the woman is established by God's creative act. The deep sleep that fell upon the man points to the truth that woman is not the man's own creation but God's completion of the man's creation. The man, indeed, by his own decision, freely accepts the woman as God's gift; yet he could no more have refused to do so than he could have chosen an animal to be his partner. "He decides," says Barth, "for the decision that is made for him. He remains human." When the man says, "This at last!" he recognizes the "I" in this "thou," a recognition which is possible only in free and responsible decision. And so God creates Man male and female. And he does it in such a way that, in the genuine exercise of his freedom, man confirms his humanity with an unequivocal "Yes!" by the acceptance of a partner as the completion of his own humanity. Because the woman is taken from the *man*, he recognizes himself in her — recognizes that he is wholly himself only in his relationship to her. But because she is taken *from* the man, he recognizes in her a distinct and separate self, another over against him; a "thou" to whom he is so related that she is unmistakably his, yet unmistakably not his — unmistakably *of* man, yet also unmistakably *not* man but woman.

In all of this account of the completion of Man's creation as male and female, the ultimate mystery of Man's dual being is not disclosed; the veil is not lifted. What is the man, what is the woman? At the biological level the answer is easy; at the psychological level, possible. But at the ultimate theological level one can frame no *a priori* definition.

> Male and female as the Man (*Mann und Frau als der Mensch*) willed and created by God and now summoned by Him and placed under His command are in themselves as much and as little capable of description (*aussprechbar and unaussprechbar*) as the human individual in his particularity over against another. Male and female being is the prototype of all I and Thou, of all individuality in which human beings (*Mensch und Mensch*) differ from and yet belong to each other.[24]

Ultimately, continues Barth, we have no right to describe or to define this specific difference. Our task is not one of definition,

24. Barth, K.D., III/4, p. 166 [150].

but obedient decision to be what God has called us to be: Man, the creature who enjoys his freedom under God in fellowship as male and female.

Addendum:
Male and Female in the Age to Come

Though it is generally said that our becoming like angels in heaven means we will no longer be male and female, what many exegetes and theologians have really meant is that there will be no females in heaven. Commenting on Jesus' view of woman, and supposedly elucidating its great advance over traditional Judaism, Oepke says:

> We never hear from the lips of Jesus a derogatory word concerning woman as such. In holding out the prospect of sexless being like that of the angels in the consummated kingdom of God (Mk. 12:25 . . .) He indirectly lifts from woman the curse of her sex and sets her at the side of man as equally the child of God.[25]

If Jesus never belittled women, the theologians, to judge from such a comment, are hardly able to follow his example.

*   *   *

Though the church has commonly understood Jesus' saying recorded in Mark 12:25 as meaning that sexuality will pass away with this life, not all theologians have agreed. Augustine first put the question of whether the bodies of women shall retain their own sex in the resurrection and answered it in the affirmative. That men will rise as men was never made a question since the answer was as self-evident to the good bishop as the axioms of Euclid. We should, however, not make this observation with too great severity. Considering his views of fallen sexuality, one is more inclined to commend the candor reflected in the answer the great theologian gave to his question concerning women than to condemn his obvious prejudice in framing it.

> From the words, "Till we all come to a perfect man, to the measure of the age of the fullness of Christ," and from the words, "Conformed to the image of the Son of God,"

25. Albrecht Oepke, "γυνή," *Theological Dictionary of the New Testament* (hereafter *TDNT*), ed. Gerhard Kittel, tr. Geoffrey Bromiley, I (Grand Rapids: Eerdmans, 1964), p. 785.

some conclude that women shall not rise women, but that all shall be men, because God made man only of earth and woman only of the man. For my part, they seem to be wiser who make no doubt that both sexes shall rise. For there shall be no lust, which is now the cause of confusion. For before they sinned, the man and the woman were naked and were not ashamed. From those bodies, then, vice shall be withdrawn while nature shall be preserved. And the sex of woman is not a vice but nature. It shall then indeed be superior to carnal intercourse and childbearing; nevertheless the female members shall remain adapted not to the old uses, but to a new beauty, which, so far from provoking lust, now extinct, shall excite praise to the wisdom and clemency of God, who both made what was not and delivered from corruption what he made. . . .

Jesus himself also, when asked by the Sadducees, who denied the resurrection, which of the seven brothers should have to wife the woman whom all in succession had taken to raise up seed to their brother, as the law enjoined, says, "Ye do err, not knowing the Scriptures nor the power of God." And though it was a fit opportunity for his saying, "She about whom you make inquiries shall herself be a man, and not a woman," he said nothing of the kind; but "in the resurrection they neither marry nor are given in marriage, but are as the angels of God in heaven."

The Lord then denied that there would be in the resurrection, not women, but marriages; and he uttered this denial in circumstances in which the question mooted would have been more easily and speedily solved by denying that the female sex should exist, if this had in truth been foreknown by him. But, indeed, he even affirmed that the sex should exist by saying, "They shall not be given in marriage," which can only apply to females; "Neither shall they marry," which applies to males. There shall therefore be those who are in this world accustomed to marry and be given in marriage, only there they shall make no such marriages.[26]

* * *

As we have observed, Jesus added to the negative, that people shall not marry in heaven, the positive, that they shall be "like the angels." Our slight knowledge of angelic beings

26. Augustine, *De civ. Dei,* XXII, 17.

would hardly warrant the conclusion that they are in no way involved in a fellowship like that of male and female. The question is best left where Milton's Raphael put it when he rebuffed
Adam's importunate curiosity about the manner in which celestial spirits express their love. Adam asks:

> Love not the heav'nly spirits, and how their love
> Express they, by looks only, or do they mix
> Irradiance, virtual or immediate touch?
> To whom the angel with a smile that glow'd
> Celestial rosie red, love's proper hue,
> Answered: "Let it suffice thee that thou know'st
> Us happy, and without love no happiness."[27]

*   *   *

Christian artists, whose vision may well be more pro-
foundly true at this point than that of the theologians, have
generally regarded the denizens of the world to come as men
and women. The great medieval representations of the resurrection and the last judgment obviously do so. In the most
famous episode in the *Divine Comedy*, Dante boldly places
Paolo and Francesca de Rimini together in hell.[28] Descending
to the second circle of Upper Hell where the souls of the lustful
are tossed upon a howling wind (the symbol of raging passion),
Dante requests of Virgil an audience with the tragic lovers and
hears Francesca lament,

> Love, that to no loved heart remits love's score,
> Took me with such great joy of him, that see!
> It holds me yet and ne'er shall leave me more.[29]

Of course an artist's vision is not to be taken as a literal
piece of scientific reporting. Dante's allegory of hell is a commentary on the soul's self-knowledge in its potential for evil
and a "revelation of the nature of impenitent sin." But if we do
not learn from the allegory, orthodox doctrine says that we will

27. Milton, *Paradise Lost*, VIII, ll. 615ff.
28. For political reasons Francesca was given in marriage to the deformed
Gianciotto, son of Malatesta da Verrucchio, lord of Rimini. She fell in love
with his younger brother Paolo and became his mistress. Having surprised
them one day together, her husband stabbed them both to death (A.D.
1285). Significantly, Dante places Gianciotto in "Cain's place," first rung
of the lowest circle of hell, far below his victims. But that is another matter.
29. Dante, *Divine Comedy*, "Hell," Canto V, ll. 103-105, tr. Dorothy
Sayers (Baltimore: Penguin Classics, 1962).

experience the reality; and it is surely difficult to see how that reality can be wholly different from our present male/female reality, as Dante's handling of matters in this place illustrates.

E. Man and Woman in Barth's Theology: An Evaluation

No one with a sense for theology can read Barth on the question of Man as male and female without admiration for his originality and his provocative insight into a subject too long in need of the grand treatment reserved to dogmatics. Barth has made it difficult for theology henceforth to treat the question of human sexuality as a footnote to the doctrine of Man. And this is a great service, especially in a day like ours when people are bombarded with "sex" in the crude, sensual, degenerate sense, an approach whose purpose is to stimulate the libido and whose effect is to offend enlightened sentiment.

Furthermore, by associating the male/female quality of human life with the discussion of the *imago*, Barth has placed it at the very center of the Christian doctrine of Man. Whether or not one finds his argument compelling in its unique aspects, one can see that it has the advantage of calling the church to frame a theology of Man which is also and at the same time a theology of woman, and there is, perhaps, no more urgent task before the church today. But more of this anon. For the moment we must address ourselves to the question: Is our human existence as male and female what it means to be in the divine image? Barth has answered in the affirmative, and in evaluating his answer the following should be noted.

If one affirms without qualification that Man's being in the divine image means his being male and female, and if the word "image" denotes "likeness" or "reflection," then obviously God in himself must be not only a fellowship of persons (Trinity), but this fellowship must somehow correspond to the specific fellowship of male and female at the human level. Barth, of course, does not believe this is so; he does not believe one can suppose that the personal fellowship in the Godhead has a sexual aspect. In fact, he does not even believe that the personal fellowship in God is that of distinct individuals, as human beings are distinct individuals. Speaking of the relational analogy (*analogia relationis*) between the Divine Being, as a fellowship of I and Thou, and Man's being, as a fellowship of male and female, he cautions:

> There can be no question of anything more than an *analogy*. The differentiation and relationship between the I and the Thou in the divine being, in the sphere of the *Elohim*, are not identical with the differentiation and relationship between male and female. That it takes this form in man, corresponding to the bisexuality of animals too, belongs to the creatureliness of man rather than the divine likeness. It also belongs to his creatureliness that the relationship between the I and the Thou in man takes place only in the form of the differentiation and relationship between two different individuals, whereas in the case of God they are included in the one individual.

> Analogy, even as the analogy of relation, does not entail likeness but the correspondence of the unlike. This correspondence of the unlike is what takes place in the fact that the being of man represents, in the form of the co-existence of the different individuals of male and female, a creaturely and therefore a dissimilar repetition of the fact that the one God is in Himself not only I but also I and Thou, i.e., I only in relation to Himself who is also Thou, and Thou only in relation to Himself who is also I. This is the God who as Creator is free for man, and the corresponding being is the man who as a creature is free for God. ["Free" here means, for Barth, "open to each other, capable of and in fellowship with each other."] This God can see, recognise and discover Himself in man. . . .[30]

To elaborate Barth's point, the doctrine of the Trinity speaks of God in the singular (he is one in essence), and Christian piety addresses God in the singular. In using the term

30. Barth, *K.D.*, III/1, p. 220 [196]. These remarks are found, as is so often the case in the *Dogmatik*, in a lengthy excursus in fine print, a location which belies their importance. In the light of these remarks, incidentally, one can appreciate why Barth as a theologian, no more than Berkouwer, would ever suggest that Gen. 1:27, read as Hebrew poetry, is saying that "in his image" is parallel to "in the image of God" which, in turn, is parallel to "male and female," so far as *meaning* is concerned.

"Person" to describe the members of the Godhead, the doctrine of the Trinity affirms that God in himself is a fellowship *like* that of three human persons; but such a fellowship of persons at the human level is only a reflection of the divine fellowship. Humans are so distinct from each other that even in the most intimate fellowship they are not one as God is one. They always remain "they," even when united as one flesh in marriage. God, on the other hand, always remains "he," even when distinguished as the three Persons of the Trinity. Hence some theologians prefer the so-called "individual" analogy of the Trinity; others, the "social" analogy.

We allude to these matters, not to probe the mysteries of the Godhead, but only to illumine the caution of the theologians. The mysterious unity in God, his oneness, is such that those theologians who see God's likeness reflected in Man as man-in-fellowship are careful not to press the analogy as though the divine fellowship of Father, Son, and Spirit were a fellowship of three Gods (tritheism).

This caution, which Barth himself (albeit in fine print) feels constrained to state, poses the question: Has Barth not overstated his case in affirming that the fellowship of male and female *is* the divine image? What his position really comes out to, it seems, is this: In God's own being there is a radical distinction; God is Father, Son, and Holy Spirit. Hence God is in himself a God who is in fellowship with himself. So also in Man's being there is a radical distinction: Man is male and female; hence Man too is a being who is in fellowship with himself. But it is an abstraction to talk of this fellowship, in Man's case, as simply a fellowship of persons, because there are no such persons in the abstract, but only persons who are men and persons who are women. At our creaturely, human level the most elemental form of fellowship we know is the fellowship of male and female, and we never know fellowship in any other way than as men and as women. Therefore, Man's existence in the fellowship of male and female is the mode of his existence as created in the image of God.

To say only this much, rather than as much as Barth sometimes says, does justice to the text of Genesis 1:27 and Genesis 5:1, 2. In the Genesis narrative it is not declared expressly that

God's creating Man in his image means he created him male and female. Yet the latter is brought into such close conjunction with the former as to imply the most intimate relation between Man's existence in the image of God and his fellowship as male and female. The two, therefore, should never be discussed separately. So far as Man is concerned, being in the divine image and being male and female, though not synonymous, are yet so closely related that one cannot speak biblically about the one without speaking also about the other, even though, surprisingly, for centuries theologians have sought to do so. Whether one blames this procedure on Greek philosophy or male self-centeredness, or both, a corrective in theological anthropology is long overdue at this point. To the centuries of understatement, then, Barth's statement, even if it be an overstatement, is a wholesome antidote.

Barth's discussion suffers, in our judgment, not only from occasional overstatement, but also from complexity — even confusion — as the argument unfolds, since he constantly shifts the subject of discourse from Man's creation as male and female to the institution of marriage with its roles of husband and wife. Barth understands well enough that these two questions are not the same, but often he speaks as though they were. Though it may be that at times the wheels of his thought slide into the well-worn ruts, this faulty workmanship is not due to an understandable tendency to fall back into the theological tradition of the centuries. Nor is it simply a matter of fidelity to Scripture with its overwhelming emphasis, especially in the Old Testament, upon marriage and the family. In the last analysis it is the result of his supralapsarian approach whereby redemption is made the ultimate purpose of creation. Since the redeemed people of God, the church, with Christ as its head, is the ultimate *telos* of creation, and since this reality, in the mysterious purpose of God, is likened to marriage (in the Old Testament Israel is the wife of Jahweh; in the New Testament the church is the bride of Christ), therefore Barth frequently speaks of the fellowship of male and female as though it were all one with that of husband and wife.

For example, Barth says that what happens in Genesis 2:18

is *not* a wedding — a highly perceptive observation.[31] Yet he cites the words of the bride in the Song of Solomon 2:16: "My beloved is mine and I am his," as the woman's answer to the man's: "This at last," in Genesis 2:23.[32] Again, he affirms that the male/female relationship is the fundamental form of human fellowship; marriage, by contrast, is a calling which not everyone receives. Yet at other times he speaks of marriage as a necessity, as when he says that one misunderstands the prophets if he supposes that their vision of God and Israel as husband and wife is simply a picture taken from the natural realm. Their thought did not move from creation to redemption; the order is the other way around. The movement is from redemption to creation; God from all eternity elected Israel, and *therefore* in the fellowship of Man in the erotic relationship of husband and wife the prophets perceived the necessary reflex, in the human sphere, of the eternal God-given covenant of grace.[33] In Barth's argument it is not always clear how this necessity of marriage is related to the freedom one has in Christ to emulate the example of our Lord in choosing the celibate life.

It is not our purpose to discuss, much less to dispute, Barth's overarching vision of the final meaning of creation, particularly the final meaning of the creation of Man as male and female.[34] We are simply observing that he fails, in his treatment of the subject, to keep the strands of the argument clearly distinct. And in doing so, he obscures the point, which needs to be made clear in our day above all others, that the Christian view of human sexuality is not all one and the same with the Christian view of marriage. The importance of this point will become increasingly evident as our discussion proceeds, since we are endeavoring to understand the whole issue of Man as a fellowship of male and female, both in creation and redemption, apart from the question of marriage, a method which would be self-defeating and contradictory were it not for the

31. Barth, K.D., III/1, pp. 373-374 [326-327]. For a detailed analysis of the second creation narrative, including Barth's comment, see below, pp. 120ff.

32. Barth, K.D., III/1, pp. 357-358 [312-313].

33. Barth, K.D., III/1, pp. 363f. [317f.].

34. For some really heady theologizing the student may look at K.D., III/2, pp. 385f. [296f.], where Barth tries to show how the Old Testament view of Man as male and female is mysteriously on target in the light of Man's sin, the atonement, etc.

distinction between human sexuality as such and the institution
of marriage and the family.[35]

35. The same limitation is found in D. S. Bailey, who, in his excellent
analysis, not only follows Barth, but goes beyond him in seeing the implications for male/female hierarchy. Bailey's statement of the *analogia relationis* is as good as any we have seen; yet he, too, illustrates the meaning
of Genesis by appealing to rabbinic pronouncements that the man who
remains unmarried is not "a whole man," "no proper person," since he
"diminishes the likeness of God." This is rather severe on Jesus. See
Bailey's *Sexual Relation in Christian Thought*, pp. 271-272.

III

The Relationship Between Man and Woman

A. *Introduction*

We have affirmed, following Barth, that Man, as created in the divine image, is Man-in-fellowship; we have further affirmed that the primary form of this fellowship is that of male and female. These affirmations imply two ineluctable obligations given with one's humanity, namely, the preservation of one's own sexual integrity and the acceptance of sexual partnership. As Barth expresses it, Man has the double obligation to live as man *or* woman and as man *and* woman. In other words, the man should always live as a man and the woman should always live as a woman. There should be no attempt to transcend our dual sexuality in terms of an Ideal Humanity, nor should we denigrate sexuality as a fracturing of our humanity, the result of the fall of Man. And, in affirming our own sex, we should accept and affirm the other sex as essential to our own, confessing that God has so created us that it is not good that we should be alone.

Because this is so, the question of relationship, specifically the man/woman relationship, becomes a central question in any theology of Man. Viewing this relationship as more fundamental than that of marriage, obviously we cannot conceive of human sexuality as simply a form of biological specialization for the purpose of reproduction. The procreative function of the sexes, important as this may be, is only one among many aspects of a complex, creative, dynamic, all-pervasive human fellowship, a fellowship which expresses itself in and through a variety of specific relationships to the benefit of both the individual and society as a whole.

49

In framing a theology of the man/woman relationship, the basic issue that has to be faced is this: Is the woman, according to the ordinance of creation, subordinate to the man? While the first creation narrative, which includes the fundamental affirmation that Man in the divine image is male and female (Gen. 1:27), contains no hint of such a hierarchical view, the second narrative (Gen. 2:18-23), which we have treated as supplementing the first, allows, if it does not actually imply, that the woman is subordinate to the man. Here we are told that the woman was created *from* and *for* the man. What is the theological significance of this? Does the fact that the man was created first imply the headship of the male? The major theologians of the church have thought so and have reinforced their understanding of this narrative by appealing to the account of the fall as found in Genesis 3.

According to the fall narrative, the woman, being first deceived by the tempter, in turn seduced the man; and so the whole human race came to ruin. Was her transgression the first instance of female insubordination? Should we conclude from this sad story of the woman's offense that her proper place is one of quiet submission to the man? In seeking an answer to this question we shall first briefly review the New Testament basis for the doctrine of sexual hierarchy and then examine the way in which theologians have understood it and argued for it in Christian theology.

B. An Examination of the New Testament Texts on Which a Hierarchical View of the Man/Woman Relationship is Based in Christian Theology

1. Introduction

The woman's natural dependency on the man as provider (hunter) and protector (warrior) throughout the millennia of human history is due to the obvious fact that, as the male of the human species, he is endowed with greater physical strength, and, as the father, with more leisure time. Such a natural dependency is compatible with the patriarchal form of society found in the Old Testament. In such a society the man is recognized as the head of the family or clan; he assumes the responsibility to provide and is invested with the authority to rule. A hierarchical view of human relationships in Christian theology is one which says that this headship of the man is a divine absolute, transcending the relativities of time and place. The primary model of all social relationships is the family, in which the woman as wife is subject to the man as husband even as the children are subject in all things to their parents. This family structure reflects God's "chain of command," which must be recognized and maintained if human society is to survive as fully human.

The pivotal texts on which such a conclusion is based are in the Pauline epistles, where all the various strands of the argument are reflected, yet not in any order that would easily rank them as primary or secondary in the apostle's mind. Some passages have to do with the creation of the woman from and for the man as recorded in Genesis 2; some have to do with the woman's part in the fall as recorded in Genesis 3; and some have to do with the behavior and dress appropriate to men and women respectively, as these illumine, in the apostle's mind, the proper role to be assumed by the male and the female. All of these considerations are viewed by Paul as indicative of the relationship which God intended to prevail between men and women.

Oftentimes, when speaking to these matters, the apostle assumes the man and the woman are related as husband and wife; but he obviously intends to speak not simply of marriage, but of marriage as it reflects the general relationship between man and woman. None of the apostle's statements implies that he thought of the woman as less the object of God's redemptive love than the man; some, however, may imply that he thought of the woman as inferior to the man; and all of them imply that he thought of the woman as subordinate to the man.

2. The Pauline Statement of the Argument

The first Pauline statement we shall consider is found in I Corinthians 11:2-16, which reads:

(2) Now I praise you that you remember me in all things

and hold fast the traditions even as I delivered them to you. (3) But I would have you know, that the head of every man is Christ; and the head of the woman is the man; and the head of Christ is God. (4) Every man praying or prophesying, having his head veiled, dishonors his head. (5) But every woman praying or prophesying with her head unveiled dishonors her head; for it is one and the same thing as if she were shaven. (6) For if a woman is not veiled, let her also be shorn; but if it is a shame to a woman to be shorn or shaven, let her be veiled. (7) For a man indeed ought not to have his head veiled, forasmuch as he is the image and glory of God; but the woman is the glory of the man. (8) For the man is not of the woman, but the woman of the man; (9) neither was the man created for the woman; but the woman for the man. (10) For this cause ought the woman to have a sign of authority on her head, because of the angels. (11) Nevertheless, neither is the woman without the man, nor the man without the woman, in the Lord. (12) For as the woman is of the man, so is the man also by the woman; but all things are of God. (13) Judge in yourselves; is it seemly that a woman pray to God unveiled? (14) Does not even nature itself teach you, that, if a man has long hair, it is a dishonor to him? (15) But if a woman has long hair it is glory to her; for her hair is given her for a covering. (16) But if any man seems to be contentious we have no such custom, neither the churches of God.

Knowing as we do that Paul's letters deal with concrete historical situations arising in the churches he had established, most scholars are of the opinion that the above remarks about women were occasioned by what might be called "the first woman's emancipation movement." At least some, if not all, of the women in the Corinthian congregation were seeking to express the equality of the sexes, implied in the Christian message that Paul had proclaimed, by laying aside their veils during the service of worship. As members of the congregation, women were praying and prophesying without any veil to cover their heads, just as did the men. This is where the problem began.

In this statement of the case, we are assuming that Paul is not thinking of the woman's exercise of devotion in the privacy of her own home. It is true that strictest Jewish custom forbade the woman to uncover her head in the presence of men, even in her own home; but it is very unlikely that the apostle, though "after the straitest sect of his religion he lived a Pharisee" (Acts 26:5), would have forced such scruples on his female converts in the Gentile world. That he is speaking to the woman's behavior in the assembled congregation, rather than in her home, is indicated by the fact that in this same chapter he goes on to discuss irregularities in the celebration of the Lord's Supper (vv. 17f.) which were obviously matters of corporate worship.

Furthermore, while the term "praying" can describe a private act at home, "prophesying" really cannot. This term refers to a public act in the assembly of the church. In the Pauline churches, to prophesy is to utter divine truth, under the immediate prompting of the Spirit, in the midst of the congregation, for the mutual edifying of those gathered together. As with those who have the gift of tongues, Paul instructs the prophets to speak in due order, sharing the time with others in a manner that all may learn and be exhorted (I Cor. 14:29f.). Hence it is certain that in I Corinthians 11 he is speaking of women who were leading the congregation in acts of worship with their heads unveiled. This removal of the veil was their offense.

As for the veil, when the first-century Jewess left her house, especially in the larger cities like Jerusalem, not only was her head covered but her face also. Both were hidden by the use of two head veils, a headband on the forehead with bands to the chin, and a hairnet with ribbons and knots, so that she could not be recognized. A woman who went out without this headdress committed such an offense to good taste that her husband had the right — indeed the duty — to put her away without paying the divorce settlement.[1]

Whether Paul was thinking of such a veiling, or one that covered only the head, is immaterial to the argument. From ancient times, in Israel as in all societies, clothes served equally to distinguish the sexes and to symbolize their mutual relation. (Hence the law forbidding a man to dress as a woman or a

1. Cf. Joachim Jeremias, *Jerusalem in the Time of Jesus* (Philadelphia: Fortress Press, 1969), pp. 359-360, with sources.

woman as a man, Deut. 22:5.) The veil is that which screens, hides, protects, covers, masks and disguises the one who wears it. It has always been associated in ancient Eastern culture with the silence of anonymity and modesty belonging to the woman. In Christian culture, the nun above all others has personified this image of the woman, so much so that the phrase "to take the veil" means to assume the cloistered life. Perceptive women have seen in the veil all that opposes their development as authentic persons. It is the sign of their hiddenness, their invisibility, their surrender to selflessness that they may achieve, not a personal, individual fulfillment, but a generic fulfillment in the role which the male has allotted to them as women. In our day nuns, who have worn the veil through the centuries in silent submission, have begun to challenge their intransigent male superiors in the ecclesiastical hierarchy over such seemingly small things as the length of their skirts and the character of their habits. They do this realizing that these small things have implications for the larger question of their right of self-determination.

Not only Catholic bishops, but Protestant theologians, have given considerable attention — in a less literal manner — to this matter of the veil. From Reformation times they have treated it as a matter of no consequence which yet, somehow, has great consequence. "What?" asks Calvin: "Does religion consist in a woman's shawl, so that it is unlawful for her to go out with a bare head?" This is of no more consequence, he declares, than whether one bends his knees when he prays.[2] Yet Paul obviously thought it of consequence, for it was the sign of the woman's subordination to the man. And Calvin, like other Protestant theologians coming after him, considered the matter of woman's subordination to be a very definite and important part of Christian doctrine in a way that belies his professed indifference to head coverings.

This subordination, Paul reasons, is a part of a larger hierarchy which reaches up to God himself. As God is the head of Christ, so Christ is the head of the man and so the man is the head of the woman (vv. 2, 3). The word "head" is used by Paul to denote the one next above one in the hier-

2. John Calvin, Institutes, IV, x, 31, tr. John Allen (Philadelphia: Presbyterian Board of Christian Education, 1936).

archy of divinely constituted authority.[3] Hence it is very important, in the apostle's thinking, that a person should understand his place in this hierarchy and reflect this understanding by conforming to the proper symbolism so far as his literal head is concerned. To violate this symbolism by covering the head during prayer, if one is a man, or by uncovering it, if one is a woman, is to deny one's place in the divinely constituted hierarchy of authority. What the woman who prayed or prophesied without her veil was doing, the veil being the symbol of her subordination to the man, was to deny in a symbolic way her subordination to the man; and that was the same thing as if the man were to deny his subordination to Christ, or if Christ were to deny his subordination to God his Father in his Messianic role as the Savior.

Paul therefore uses very strong language. The man who prays or prophesies having his head covered dishonors his head;[4] while the woman who prays or prophesies having her head uncovered dishonors her head. It is as though the man, symbolically, were to subordinate himself to the woman while the woman, symbolically, were to deny her subordination to the man. So to act would confuse the relationship which God has established between the sexes.[5]

Such a view of the relationship of the sexes, for Paul, would be contrary to nature as God has structured it by the ordinance of creation. Nature itself teaches us that for a man to have long hair is a dishonor to him, but for a woman it is a glory, for her long hair is the natural counterpart of the

3. Probably the Greek κεφαλή, as here used, is virtually synonymous with ἀρχή, meaning "origin" or "first cause." The female's ontological inferiority, in the apostle's thought, is grounded in the male's priority of creation. The woman is *of* the man; he is her "first cause." See Bailey, *Sexual Relation in Christian Thought*, pp. 295f.

4. The text (v. 4) says literally: "Every man praying or prophesying having down from the head [κατὰ κεφαλῆς ἔχων, i.e. having a veil hanging down from the head] dishonors his head."

5. Some interpret this passage as follows: Every man praying . . . having his (literal) head covered dishonors his (figurative) head, i.e. Christ, since he wears on his literal head the sign of subordination to another human being, when in reality, as a Christian man, he is subordinate to Christ only; every woman praying with her (literal) head uncovered dishonors her (figurative) head, i.e. her husband, since, by removing her veil, she refuses the sign of subordination to her husband. This interpretation is somewhat obtuse. The ultimate thrust of the passage remains, however, the same.

veil; it is given her for a covering. ("She as a veil down to the slender waist, her unadorned golden tresses wore," sings Milton of Eve in *Paradise Lost*.) For a woman to take off her veil, then, is the same as if she were to be shaven or shorn; and that would be a shame to any woman.

This sense of nature which teaches us that an uncovered head dishonors a woman is for the apostle simply the awareness, at the level of consciousness, of the truth which God himself embedded in our humanity when he created man and woman in the beginning. The man is "the image and glory of God" and the woman is "the glory of the man." Paul probably omits to say that the woman is the *image* of the man, lest his readers conclude that she is not the image of God. That would be more than he wants to say, since the woman like the man is created in the divine image. But the woman is not so directly in the image as the man; she is the glory of the man who is the image and glory of God.

The term "glory" ($\delta\acute{o}\xi a$) is used of that which honors, magnifies and brings praise to one. The man is so in the divine image as to bring honor and praise to God; the woman, as to bring honor and praise to the man. Obviously the man cannot bring honor and praise to God, as he ought, if he subordinates himself to the woman by covering his head; nor can the woman bring honor and praise to the man as she ought if, by removing the veil from her head, she refuses to subordinate herself to the man.[6]

And how do we know that God created the woman to be the man's glory? We know this from the account of the creation of the man and the woman in Genesis 2. The man, says the apostle, is not of the woman, but the woman of the man; neither was the man created for the woman, but the woman for the man (vv. 8, 9). For this cause ought the woman to have the sign of authority on her head.[7]

At this juncture in the argument a curious detail is added.

6. The custom whereby the Jewish man prayed with his head covered, as a mark of reverence and sorrow, did not begin until the fourth century and hence was unknown to the apostle.

7. Literally: "The woman ought to have authority on her head" ($\dot{o}\phi\epsilon\acute{\iota}\lambda\eta$ $\dot{\eta}$ $\gamma\upsilon\nu\grave{\eta}$ $\dot{\epsilon}\xi o\upsilon\sigma\acute{\iota}a\nu$ $\ddot{\epsilon}\chi\epsilon\iota\nu$ $\dot{\epsilon}\pi\grave{\iota}$ $\tau\hat{\eta}\varsigma$ $\kappa\epsilon\phi a\lambda\hat{\eta}\varsigma$), a difficult reading which is best interpreted by supplying some such term as "sign," "mark," "symbol."

The woman is to have the sign of authority on her head, says the apostle, "on account of the angels." This reference to angels is so obscure that expositors can only conjecture as to what the text may mean. Probably Paul has in mind the Greek rendition of Psalm 138:1 where allusion is made to angels in a context of worship. In keeping with this view, this verse has been traditionally understood to refer to the good angels invisibly present and silently participating when the saints gather to worship.[8] If this is the thought, then it would be an added incentive to Christian women to refrain from any impropriety in the gathered assembly which might offer an offense to these denizens of the celestial realm.[9]

Whatever obscurity one may feel in the reference to angels, such obscurity does not affect the plain meaning of Paul's argument as a whole as he sets it forth in I Corinthians 11. The subordination of the woman to the man is an essential part of the hierarchy which God himself has established to insure a proper order in the relationships of life. Even the parenthetical remark that the woman is of the man and the man through the woman (vv. 11-12) does not alter the substance of the apostle's reasoning. It does, however, constitute something of a counterbalance. Although the first woman owed her existence to the man from whom she was taken, all other men owe their existence to the women who conceived them and brought them into the world. The man, then, should not think only of his priority over the woman, but also of his dependence upon her in the divine order, since this dependence is also the will of God from whom are all things.[10]

The same view of female subordination to the male elaborated in I Corinthians 11 is found in Paul's letter to the Ephe-

8. See the *Te Deum*: "To thee all angels cry holy, holy, holy; together with the glorious company of the apostles, the goodly fellowship of the prophets, the noble army of martyrs and the holy church throughout all the world," etc.

9. Some commentators substitute for the possibility of offense that of temptation, supposing that Paul is alluding to Genesis 6:1f., where reference is made to the sons of God (angels?) taking to wife the beautiful daughters of men. Women should not, by the immodest behavior of removing their head covering, tempt (after the example of ancient times) the "sons of God" who are present in the worshipping assembly. This, however, seems a farfetched interpretation.

10. For further comment on I Corinthians 11, including vv. 11-12, see below, "The Pauline Argument Revisited," pp. 111ff.

sians, chapter 5, verses 22-33. This passage, similar in content
to the Corinthians passage, is more familiar because of its
traditional use in the marriage ceremony of the church.

(22) Wives, be in subjection unto your own husbands, as
unto the Lord. (23) For the husband is the head of the
wife, as Christ also is the head of the church, being himself the Savior of the body. (24) But as the church is
subject to Christ, so let the wives also be to their husbands
in everything.

(25) Husbands, love your wives, even as Christ also loved
the church, and gave himself up for it; (26) that he might
sanctify it, having cleansed it by the washing of water with
the word, (27) that he might present the church to himself a glorious church, not having spot or wrinkle or any
such thing; but that it should be holy and without blemish.
(28) Even so ought husbands also to love their own wives
as their own bodies. He who loves his own wife loves
himself: (29) for no man ever hated his own flesh; but
nourishes and cherishes it, even as Christ also the church;
(30) because we are members of his body. (31) For this
cause shall a man leave his father and mother, and shall
cleave to his wife; and the two shall become one flesh.
(32) This mystery is great: but I speak in regard of Christ
and of the church. (33) Nevertheless do you also severally
love each one his own wife even as himself; and let the wife
see that she fear her husband.

In this passage, the hierarchy of authority is drawn on a
lesser canvas than in I Corinthians: Christ's subjection to God
is not mentioned, and on the human plane express reference is
made only to the subjection of the wife to the husband, not of
the woman to the man as such. But the theological thrust is
the same. In fact, within the limitations of the marriage bond,
one can hardly conceive of a more clear and emphatic statement of hierarchy. Even the term used to describe the ideal
relationship of a Christian husband to his wife is different
from that used to describe the wife's relationship to her husband. While the husband is to love (ἀγαπάω) his wife, the
wife is to fear (φοβέω) her husband. This fear, to be sure, is
not the cowering fear of a slave; it is rather the reverential
respect which informs a woman's love for her husband as the
authoritative head of the family. As the love which Christians

have for the exalted Lord, the Head of the Church, is mingled with reverence (the fear of the Lord is the beginning of wisdom), so, by analogy, is the love of a wife for her husband who is her head, her "lord" as Chaucer's immortal Grieselda owned her husband to be.[11] Obviously, then, the marriage relation is not a matter of mutuality as between equal partners. While the apostle might well have said: "Wives, love your husbands," he would never have said: "Husbands, *fear* your wives."[12]

Similar sentiments are expressed also in Colossians 3:18-19, where Paul admonishes wives to be in subjection to their husbands and husbands to love their wives; in I Timothy 2:11, a passage which instructs women to learn in quietness with all subjection; in Titus 2:5, which urges older women to teach the younger women to be in subjection to their husbands that the word of God be not blasphemed; and in I Peter 3:1f., which urges wives to be in subjection to their husbands, even if they are unbelievers, that the husbands may be won over by their meek and quiet spirit. In displaying such a spirit, Christian women emulate the example of the holy women of old, like Sarah, who obeyed Abraham, calling him lord. In these passages there are also references to modest apparel as becoming a Christian woman and to simplicity of hair style (I Tim. 2:9; I Peter 3:3), though the argument is not elaborated as in I Corinthians 11.

Besides the order of creation ("man is not created from the woman but woman from the man"), we find one other item in the New Testament argument for the woman's subjection to the man, though (happily) it is not emphasized. It

11. Geoffrey Chaucer, "The Clerk's Tale," *Canterbury Tales.* It is interesting, in this regard, to note that in Pentecostal communions women have full liberty to speak in church, I Cor. 14 and I Tim. 2 to the contrary notwithstanding. But as wives they are definitely subordinate to their husbands according to Eph. 5. The author recalls listening on a Sunday morning to such a Pentecostal woman pastor in a small mining town where her husband was the mill superintendent. The place where she exercised *her* calling was determined by the place where her husband exercised *his.*

12. Admittedly some modern translations of the text soften the meaning sufficiently to make such a reversal possible. For example: "Let the wife . . . respect her husband" (New American Standard Version); "the woman must see to it that she pays her husband all respect" (New English Bible). The apostle surely believed that the husband should also "respect" the wife. Thus there is achieved a mutuality in translation not felt in the original text.

concerns the woman's part in the fall as recorded in Genesis 3. In I Corinthians 14:33b-35, we read:

> As in all the churches of the saints, let the women keep silence in the churches: for it is not permitted unto them to speak; but let them be in subjection as also says the law. And if they would learn anything, let them ask their own husbands at home; for it is shameful for a woman to speak in the church.

To the same effect, and more explicitly still, I Timothy 2:11-15 tells us why it is shameful for a woman to speak in the church.

> Let a woman learn in quietness with all subjection. But I permit not a woman to teach, nor to have dominion over a man, but to be in quietness. For Adam was first formed, then Eve; and Adam was not deceived, but the woman, being deceived, has fallen into transgression. But she shall be saved through her childbearing, if they continue in faith and love and sanctification with sobriety.

This last sentence may mean that the woman, though she was first in transgression, will yet obtain the grace of salvation through her bearing of the Child, i.e. the Savior who is the woman's seed (Gen. 3:15), if they, i.e. the man and the woman as husband and wife, continue in faith, and so forth. But more likely, as virtually all translations suggest, this verse means that the woman, though she was the prime mover in the fall and therefore under a curse in childbearing (Gen. 3:16), will be brought safely through the threatening experience of motherhood, if they, i.e. women, continue to live a life becoming the Christian name.

Whatever one may say about the exact meaning of this last difficult sentence, the main thrust of the passage seems clear enough. Women, according to the author, are to take a subordinate role to men in the teaching office of the church. While men may teach women, women should not aspire to reverse this relationship, for they are inferior in their gifts, so far as the teaching office is concerned. This inferiority is inferred from the fact that the male (Adam) was created first; and it is an inference for which the author of I Timothy finds corroboration in the further fact that the woman, not the man, was approached and seduced by the tempter. The thought seems to be that the tempter approached the woman because he knew that she did not have the same critical acumen as the man. In this, the author of I Timothy assumes, the tempter was correct since the woman, not the man, was deceived and so found in the way of transgression (v. 14). Then follows the comforting word to his feminine readers to which reference has already been made.[13]

We now have before us a complete summary of the New Testament passages on which the doctrine of woman's subordination is based. The woman is subject to the man because the man, as created first, is directly in the image and glory of God, whereas the woman, created after the man and for him, is the glory of the man. Because of her lesser endowment (presumably) she was deceived by the tempter when the man was not. Therefore she should never aspire to teach the man, but always learn from him in subjection and quiet humility. Specifically, this means that Christian women are not permitted to speak in church; in fact it would be shameful were they to do so. Therefore let them study a becoming silence.

C. The Hierarchical View of the Man/Woman Relationship Elaborated and Defended

1. A Classical Statement: Thomas Aquinas

In examining the Scriptural basis for the view that the woman is subordinate to the man, we noted that in the Pauline epistles this conclusion is inferred from the account of the woman's creation in Genesis 2 and her seduction in Genesis 3. These themes are taken up by St. Thomas in his *Summa Theologica*, First Part, Question XCII. In this section Thomas

13. The notion that women lack the critical perception to instruct men is sometimes fortified by listing all the female heretics from Priscilla and Maximilla to Mary Baker Eddy, a method which yields impressive results because of its selectivity. One shudders to think what the same approach to church history would do to the image of the male as a teacher of moral and religious truths!

treats of "The Production (Creation) of the Woman" in four
articles. Article One puts the question: "Whether the Woman
Should Have Been Made in the First Production of Things?"
The answer is given in the affirmative, but the very putting of
the question anticipates the pejorative approach of the whole
subsequent discussion. No such question is raised when speaking of the creation of the man; obviously he belonged to the
first production of things. In fact *he* is the crown of that first,
pristine, unfallen creation along with the stars and the seas, the
plants and the animals, all of which God pronounced good.
But the creation of the woman is another matter. There is
evidently some reason to wonder whether she belongs on the
side of the original good creation or came in with the thorns
and thistles that cover the ground and with the serpents that
crawl on their bellies and eat dust.

The arguments for the latter position, reviewed by Thomas,
are: (1) the female, as Aristotle observed, is a misbegotten
male; (2) the woman, as cursed, is subject to the man and by
nature less strong and dignified than he; and (3) she occasioned
man's fall into sin. How could a creature that is defective,
unequal in strength, dignity and honor, and the occasion of
man's moral turpitude, belong to that original primal creation
described as good?

The Angelic Doctor answers these arguments by quoting
the Scripture which says that "it is not good that the man should
be alone," from which he infers the necessity for the woman's
creation in the original order of things to assist the man ". . .
not indeed, as a helpmate in other works, as some say, since a
man can be more efficiently helped by another *man* in other
works, but as a helper in the work of generation."

Observing that in the lower orders of living things, as in
the seed of a plant, for example, the active and passive gener-
ative powers are united, Thomas goes on to say: "Among perfect animals the active power of generation belongs to the
male sex and the passive power to the female." Furthermore,
the male and the female are not in continual union but come
together only in coition, and this is especially true of Man since
he is destined to the far nobler vital action of "understanding."
Thomas admits that the woman, as regards her particular nature (female), is indeed misbegotten, since the active force in

the male seed tends to the production of a perfect male like-ness. But as to her universal nature (humanity) the woman is not misbegotten but included in nature's original intention as ordered to the work of procreation, according to the will of the Creator who formed both the male and the female.

As for the objection that the woman could not have been created in the original production of things because she is subject to rather than equal with the man, Thomas replies as follows:

> Subjection is two-fold. One is servile, by virtue of which a superior makes use of a subject for his own benefit, and this kind of subjection began after sin. There is another kind of subjection, which is called economic or civil, where-by the superior makes use of his subjects for their own benefit and good; and this kind of subjection existed even before sin. For good order would have been wanting in the human family if some were not governed by others wiser than themselves. So by such a kind of subjection woman is naturally subject to man, because in man the discretion of reason predominates. Nor is inequality among men ex-cluded by the state of innocence, as we shall prove.[14]

This paragraph is significant because it grounds man's super-ordination to the woman in ontology; by definition the male is the one in whom the "discretion of reason predominates." There-fore the woman, per definitionem, is subject to the man.

The third and final objection to regarding woman as a part of the original creation, namely that she was the occasion

14. Summa Theologica, as translated in Great Books of the Western World, ed. Robert M. Hutchins (Chicago: Encyclopaedia Britannica, 1957), XIX, p. 489. The concept of a "two-fold" subjection, one for the good of the woman as ordained by the Creator and one which enslaves the woman as a curse for her transgressions, is necessary, if one construes the second creation narrative of Genesis as implying the subordination of the woman. Calvin observes (Commentary on I Timothy) that there would seem to be a contradiction in saying that the subjection of the woman is both the imposition of her creation and the punishment of her transgression. He proposes a voluntary subjection of the woman as created, which becomes less voluntary after the fall. Later commentators have followed this lead, deploring the despotic rule of the man which crushes the woman while advocating an enlightened rule over her, informed by love, according to the alleged intent of the original creation ordinance.

of sin in the man, Aquinas answers, without denying the charge, as follows:

> If God had deprived the world of all those things which proved an occasion of sin, the universe would have been imperfect. Nor was it fitting for the common good to be destroyed in order that individual evil might be avoided, especially as God is so powerful that He can direct any evil to a good end.[15]

In Article Two, Thomas puts the question: "Whether Woman Should Have Been Made from Man?" To this question he also gives an affirmative answer citing the following reasons: (1) that the first man might be given a certain dignity as the principle of the whole human race; (2) that the man might love the woman the more knowing her to be fashioned from himself; (3) that man and woman, being united in domestic life, in which the man is the head of the woman, the woman might be made out of man as out of her principle; (4) that the truth may be set forth as in a sacrament that the church takes her origin from Christ, as the apostle says in Ephesians 5:32.

In Article Three, "Whether the Woman Was Fittingly Made from the Rib of Man?" Thomas answers: It was right for the woman to be made from a rib of man. The reason given is that this way of producing the woman signifies the social union of man and woman. For the woman should neither use authority over the man, and so she was not made from his head; nor was it right for her to be subject to man's contempt as his slave, and so she was not made from his feet. Here he stops, coming short of the affirmation of woman's partnership, since a partnership of equals is obviously not compatible with a view of hierarchical relationship in which the woman is subordinate to the man as his inferior.

One element in this "classic" statement of woman's subordination to man is largely a matter of past history. We refer to the notion that the woman, in her specific female nature, is defective (misbegotten as Thomas says), that is, less endowed with the discretion of reason so that she was deceived by the tempter. This position having been generally discredited, we

15. *Summa Theologica* XIX, p. 489.

may leave the arguments given in its support with a few terminal remarks of an historical character.[16] According to St. Thomas, since the active powers of generation belong to the male and since the first man was the principle of the whole human race, had only Eve sinned, Adam's children would not have inherited the taint of original sin; had only Adam sinned, they would have. Assuming this view, the Schoolmen laid great weight on Adam's sin because of its consequences. Yet they tended to be more lenient with the man than with the woman since Eve sinned against herself, her husband and her God, while Adam sinned only against himself and his God. Eve's sin was more grievous as she was moved with an envious desire to be like God, whereas Adam sinned by consenting to his wife out of conjugal love and fidelity. Others reached a more balanced conclusion: Adam sinned more grievously as the *cause* of damnation in his posterity, Eve the more grievously as the *occasion* of this damnation.

But all were agreed that the tempter approached the woman as the "weaker vessel."[17] It never dawned on any of the Schoolmen that this was a stereotype made plausible by the deprivations of the woman's environment; for them it was clearly a matter of ontology. They seem not to have felt in the least the absurdity in their portrayal of the woman as both the dull-witted creature who was easily duped by the devil, and the one who accomplished with ease the ruin of the man which the tempter himself was not clever enough to bring off.

This "paradox" of female stupidity and subtlety lingers on even to the present day, but it is really nonsense. We have paradox when we do not fully understand; we have nonsense when we do not wish to understand. The asymmetry between the biblical data and the view which blames the woman for the fall may be seen in the fact that in the Bible it is *fallen* Adam seeking an *alibi* who blamed the woman for his folly. In fact,

16. See also "First Addendum: Misogyny in Western Thought," pp. 149ff.
17. This phrase ("weaker vessel") from the admonition of I Pet. 3:7 to husbands to bestow honor, literally, "on the weaker vessel, the female one" (ὡς ἀσθενεοτέρῳ σκεύει τῷ γυναικείῳ), has traditionally been understood to imply the woman's lesser powers of understanding and discernment. Modern commentators tend to stress the woman's physical, or more precisely muscular, weakness in contrast to the male. While this latter was perhaps included in the author's thought, the context (3:1f.) hardly indicates that it was his primary point. The traditional understanding is most likely correct, though it is less palatable.

since she who urged him to eat of the forbidden tree was "the woman whom thou gavest to be with me" (Gen. 3:12), really God was to blame, according to Adam. In this respect the theological tradition is little more than an elaboration of Adam's original attempt to expound the truth by obscuring it.

2. A Transitional Statement: Luther and Calvin

The abandonment of the notion that the woman is an inferior variety of the human species was not achieved all at once at the time of the Protestant Reformation. The Reformers, as we know, were children of their times in many respects, and Luther especially retained unenlightened views of the role of the woman in her relationship to the man. Woman's principal task was to bear children (the traditional view that she is man's helper in the work of generation) and to relieve the sexual appetite of the fallen male. He took an emphatic view of her subjection to the man in all things. A letter of advice to his friend Stephen Roth begins: "Grace and peace in Christ and authority over your wife." Expounding Ecclesiastes 7:26, he says:

> Men are commanded to rule and to reign over their wives and families. But if woman, forsaking her position (*officio*), presumes to rule over her husband, she then and there engages in a work for which she was not created, a work which stems from her failing (*vitio*) and is evil. For God did not create this sex to rule.

> For this reason domination by women is never a happy one. The history of the Amazons, celebrated by Greek writers, might be advanced against this view. They are reported to have held the rule and to have conducted wars. But I believe what is told of them to be a fable. To be sure, the Ethiopians chose women to be both queens and princesses, in accordance with their custom, as the Ethiopian queen Candace mentioned in Acts 8:27. But this was stupid of them. . . . There is no divine permission for ruling by a woman. It may, of course, happen that she is placed in the position of a king and is given the rule; but she always has a senate of prominent men according to whose counsel all is administered. Therefore even though a woman may be put in the place of a king, this does not

confirm the rule of woman; for the text is clear: "Thy desire shall be to thy husband, and he shall rule over thee" (Gen. 3:16).[18]

Woman was created for the benefit (usum) of man, that is, for the prudent and sensible training of children. Everyone does best when he does that for which he was created. A woman handles a child better with her smallest finger than a man does with both hands. Therefore let everyone stick to that work to which God has called him and for which he was created.[19]

Luther seems to have perceived, albeit dimly, that his theory of the woman's incapacity to rule and to exercise spiritual oversight did not fit well with his doctrine of the universal priesthood of believers. In any case he allowed that the woman might assume the office of ministry by way of exception in times of necessity.[20]

Calvin took a somewhat higher ground, arguing that the woman's relation to the man was primarily social rather than procreative. She was not given the man as a "remedy" for his concupiscence, the comrade merely of his bedchamber, but to share life with him as his inseparable companion.

Calvin also rejected the age-old propensity to blame the woman as dull of understanding. Commenting on I Timothy 2:14, "Adam was not deceived, but the woman, being deceived, was found in transgression," he says: "By these words Paul does not mean that Adam was not involved in the same diabolical deception, but only that the cause and source of his deception came from Eve."[21] In other words, Eve was deceived directly by the tempter, but then Adam's turn came; he too was deceived by the evil one, yet indirectly through his wife. While this interpretation is a bit strained, it may be regarded as something of an antidote to the shameful disparagement of the woman indulged in comments on this passage by Calvin's predecessors.

18. Note how Luther here equates the curse of Gen. 3 with the ordinance of creation.
19. As quoted in *What Luther Says*, by Ewald M. Plass (St. Louis: Concordia, 1959), p. 1458.
20. See Bailey, *Sexual Relation in Christian Thought*, p. 173.
21. John Calvin, *Commentary on I Timothy*, in *Calvin's New Testament Commentaries*, ed. D. W. and T. F. Torrance (Grand Rapids: Eerdmans, 1964), X, p. 217.

However, though Calvin's views of woman harbingered better things, he held like Luther to the doctrine of female subordination, not only in marriage but in all things, especially in the oversight of the church. Commenting on I Timothy 2:12, he argues that the woman is prevented from holding the teaching office because it would not be compatible with her status as subject to the man. He sees no absurdity in a man's obeying in one relationship and commanding in another.

> But this does not apply to women who by nature are born to obey, for all wise men have always rejected γυναικοκρατίαν, the government of women, as a natural monstrosity. Thus for a woman to usurp the right to teach would be a sort of mingling of heaven and earth. Wherefore the apostle bids them to be silent and abide within the limits of their sex.[22]

Calvin makes it plain that the woman's subordination is not simply the result of the fall; by the very order of creation woman is subject to man. God did not create two "heads" of equal standing. The woman was created later to be "a kind of appendage"; she was given to the man as "a lesser helpmeet." Hence the apostle is right in reminding us of this order of creation whereby "God's eternal and inviolable appointment is clearly displayed."[23]

Fuming in Dieppe, his return to Scotland impeded by Mary, Queen of Scots, John Knox spelled out the implications of his Calvinistic training about women's place with an explicitness that left nothing to be desired. His *First Blast of the Trumpet Against the Monstrous Regiment of Women* begins with the proposition:

> To promote a woman to bear rule, superiority, dominion or empire above any nation, realm or city, is repugnant to nature; contumely to God, a thing most contrarious to his revealed will and approved ordinance; and finally it is the subversion of good order, of all equity and justice.[24]

22. Calvin, *Commentary*, p. 217.
23. Calvin, *Commentary*, pp. 217-218.
24. See *The Works of John Knox*, ed. David Laing (Edinburgh: John Thin, 1895), IV, pp. 365f. This piece of polemical writing, which won the fiery reformer the lasting resentment of Elizabeth, should be balanced by a reading of his tender and affectionate "Epistles to Mrs. Elizabeth Bower and Her Daughter Marjory," Knox's mother-in-law and wife respectively, *ibid.*, III, pp. 333f.

3. A Contemporary Statement: Karl Barth

Today no responsible theologian would say that the woman is a "kind of appendage" or "lesser helpmeet" to the man, yet the doctrine of hierarchy is still affirmed. Even Karl Barth, whose thinking in this whole area points in the direction of the full equality of the man and the woman in the fellowship of life, yet argues for female subordination. To review Barth's argument for sexual hierarchy, therefore, focuses the question: Is it possible to abandon the traditional thesis that the woman is inferior to the man and yet make a case for her subordination to him?

Instead of the view that the woman is inferior, Barth stresses the fact that she is *different*. Now it is an important point, all would agree, that men and women are different, since there can be no fellowship where there are no differences. Difference makes for mutual enrichment; and the difference between the male and the female is the primal difference in our common humanity, a difference which conditions at every level the fellowship of human life. To be male *or* female, male *and* female, is the fundamental form of our humanity. No one ever stated this more eloquently than Barth:

> At this point [where one is speaking of the radicals of I-thou fellowship] the reference cannot be to parents and children, to brothers and sisters and other relatives, to friends, to Europeans and Asiatics, to Semites and Arians, to old and young, to gifted and ungifted, to rulers and subjects, teachers and scholars, rich and poor, or even the basic distinction of individual and individual. Or rather, this basic distinction, the differentiation and connexion of I and thou, must be explained as coincident with that of male and female. All other relationships are involved in this as the original relationship. All other aspects of humanity are included in this centre.[25]

This all-pervasive, all-important difference, continues Barth, means that there can never be male life nor female, closed in on itself, sufficient unto itself. In obedience to the divine command the man must live as coordinated with, belonging to,

25. Barth, *K.D.*, III/2, § 45, p. 353 [292-293].

and turned toward the woman, and the woman must live as coordinated with, belonging to, and turned toward the man.[26]

But this all adds up to equality with a difference; and the difference cannot be such as to invalidate the equality. Barth, at times, spells this conclusion out in so many words, even when one would hardly expect it. He declares, for example, that the mutual partnership of man and woman is a parable, at the level of creation, of our partnership with God in the covenant of grace. The common element (tertium comparationis), however, consists solely in the fellowship existing between two distinct partners. Here the comparison ceases. In the God-Man relationship everything is one-sided, since all the authority and rule is on God's side, all the need and receiving on Man's side. But in the man-woman relationship everything is two-sided, since it is a matter of giving and receiving between two partners who are of like being and worth.[27]

Again, the difference between man and woman is structural and functional, says Barth. "But let one note: it is only a structural and functional difference. There is no question as to whether man and woman are both human." This structural, functional difference, continues Barth, is indeed a radical difference that points to a radical relationship. The closest, most self-evident and universally valid of all relationships, the relationship whereby the woman is to the man, and the man to the woman, that other human being, the one who is the fellow human being — this closest of all relationships is the relationship which supposes this deepest of all differences.

26. Barth, K.D., III/4, § 54, p. 181 [163]. Barth here speaks of Zuordnung, Zugehörigkeit, Zuwendung.

27. Barth, K.D., III/2, § 54, pp. 386-387 [320-321]. Were Barth consistent in limiting the univocal element (as he does here) in the analogy between Christ and the church on the one hand and husband and wife on the other to a fellowship existing between two distinct partners, there could be no objection to his supralapsarian or christocentric interpretation of Genesis in the light of Ephesians. The argument, as such, appears a good one to us. Hence we offer no criticism of it in principle, but only in the particular point of inconsistent application. To limit the tertium comparationis to a fellowship of distinct partners and at the same time broaden it to include the subordination of one partner to the other is palpably inconsistent. For further comment on Ephesians 5, see below, pp. 137ff.

But what Barth needs to show is how the fact that the woman is *different* from the man implies that she is *subordinate* to him, without concluding that the difference involves her inferiority. The concept of hierarchy, to be sure, does not in itself entail superiority and inferiority, but only that some are *over*, others are *under*; some *exercise* authority, others *submit* to it. But how can one defend a sexual hierarchy whereby men are over women — not just *some* men over *some* women, but *all* men over *all* women, because men are men and women are women — without supposing that the half of the human race which exercises authority is superior in some way to the half which submits? Classically, as we have observed, theologians did not hesitate to draw this conclusion; they based the woman's submission to the man on her inferiority. In the light of this venerable theological tradition, with which Barth is perfectly familiar, it is instructive to trace his thinking on the matter of female subordination through the third volume of his *Dogmatics*.

In III/1, Barth's understanding of I Corinthians 11:7 (where Paul declares that the man is the image and glory of God; the woman, the glory of the man) reflects his supralapsarian or Christocentric approach. According to this approach, the creation is the "external basis" of the covenant of grace and the covenant of grace is the "internal basis" of creation. In other words, the ultimate purpose of creation is redemption in Christ. Therefore, the primal confrontation and conjunction of man and woman, wherein the divine image consists, must find its true fulfillment in Jesus Christ, who according to the New Testament is the true "image of God" (II Cor. 4:4; Col. 1:15). If we perceive that Jesus Christ is the meaning and goal of Israel's covenant history, then of course he is the answer to the enigma of Genesis 1:26f., which speaks of God's creating Man "in his image."

There is, in other words, not just the "first" Adam, who is only a copy and imitation of the prototype; but also the "second" Adam, who is the reality itself.

> According to I Cor. 11:7 there is a man who actually *is* the εἰκὼν καὶ δόξα θεοῦ and from this standpoint the same can be said of every man. And side by side with

this man there is a woman who is His δόξα as He (the
Head of the woman but not without her!) is the δόξα of
God, and from the standpoint of this woman, or rather
of her husband, the same can be said of every woman. . . .
If we are to understand this [that Paul regarded the man
Jesus as the real image of God], we must not overlook the
fact that according to I Cor. 11:7 Paul always thought of
the man who is God's εἰκὼν καὶ δόξα (even in passages
where this is not immediately obvious) in conjunction
with his wife, and therefore of Jesus, not as an isolated
figure, but as *Israel's* Christ, the Head of *His community*.[28]

Obviously this tack in Barth's reasoning leads to a man/
woman hierarchy with a vengeance, since the Woman, who is
the "glory" of the second Adam, is the church of which he,
the Messiah, is the Head. How can one possibly say that every
man is the image and glory of God and every woman the glory
of the man "from this standpoint," indeed, especially from this
standpoint, without subordinating the woman to the man as
his inferior?

Barth makes a commendable but hardly convincing effort
to answer this question; he endeavors to show how the woman
is subordinate to the man, as is the church to Christ, though
equal to him as a person. He reasons as follows:

The simplest and most comprehensive definition of woman
is that she is the being to which man, himself becoming
male, can and must say in the exercise of his freedom
that "this" is now the "help corresponding to him" ("*Hilfe,
die ihm ein Gegenüber sei*") which otherwise he had sought
in vain but which had now been fashioned and brought
by God.[29]

This does not mean, insists Barth, that she is man's property,
less a human being than he. Then comes the inevitable qualification:

The fact that the relationship is not one of reciprocity
and equality, that man was not taken out of woman but
woman out of man, that primarily he does not belong to
her but she to him, and that he thus belongs to her only

28. Barth, *K.D.*, III/1, pp. 228-29 [203].
29. Barth, *K.D.*, III/1, p. 343 [300-301].

secondarily, must not be misunderstood. The supremacy of man is not a question of value, dignity or honour, but of order. It does not denote a higher humanity of man. Its acknowledgment is no shame to woman. On the contrary, it is an acknowledgment of her glory, which in a particular and decisive respect is greater even than that of man. . . . She is his glory as he himself is the glory of God (I Cor. 11:7). . . . It is the peculiar glory of her creation, i.e., that she was "taken out of man," that she completes the creation of man from man himself and that this is crowned by his own recognition and confession — it is this distinction — insurpassable in its own way, which, not for her humiliation but her exaltation, specifically and inexorably assigns her to this position. Only in this position does she possess her true humanity, but in this position she really does possess it.[30]

According to this remarkable argument, although the woman is the glory of the man who is the glory of God, her glory is the greater because the man could not be the glory of God without her who is his glory. The woman's subordination, then, becomes not humiliation but exaltation!

To justify this paradoxical view, Barth appeals to the puzzling "therefore" of Genesis 2:24: "*Therefore* shall the man leave his father and mother and shall cleave to his wife." In the marriage relationship, by God's will and plan, the man becomes the seeking, desiring, sacrificing one; the *weaker* one, if you will, who finds his fulfillment in his relationship to the woman. Without such seeking and finding, his own humanity would remain defective. Hence the entire supremacy of the man aims at this one goal, that he should submit himself to this arrangement. It is only in this humiliation, as the weaker party confronting the woman, that man can be her lord, the stronger party. Hence the woman, in reality and practice, has nothing to fear from the male's preeminence.[31]

So long, argues Barth, as the subordination of the woman was viewed in this way, as it was, indeed, in creation, it involved no humiliation. But once the relationship of the man and the woman *to God* was disturbed by sin, then their relation-

---

30. Barth, K.D., III/1, pp. 345-346 [301-303].
31. Barth, K.D., III/1, pp. 348-350 [304-306].

ship *to each other* was also disturbed. Their humanity became abstract masculinity on the one side and abstract femininity on the other, leading to the conflict of a blind dominion on the man's part and a jealous zeal for emancipation on the woman's part.[32] Advocating a return to the creation ordinance of the man's preeminence without tyranny and the woman's submission without humiliation, Barth concludes his exposition of the man/woman hierarchy in *Dogmatik*, III/1.

It would appear that the final word has yet to be spoken. We expect that he will have more to say, and when we turn to *Dogmatik*, III/2, we are not disappointed in this expectation. In this volume the fundamental conclusions drawn in III/1 are reiterated and elaborated with a somewhat different emphasis. Again the discussion centers on I Corinthians 11:2-16.

Since the man is not without the woman nor the woman without the man, in the Lord (vv. 11, 12), the question of the proper *order* in the man/woman relationship is not *per se* a large one, says Barth. But it takes on significance in the apostle's thinking because in Corinth there was an attempt to solve this question in a way that was against apostolic authority, as though freedom in Christ could reverse the order of ministry that existed between the apostle and the community. The Corinthians apparently felt in some respects quite self-sufficient (4:8), and hence Paul refers briefly to this issue in chapter 11, verses 1 and 2, with an admonition and a commendation. Were Paul to have yielded in the slightest his relative human authority as an apostle, it would have compromised the absolute authority of Jesus whose witness Paul was. And without the sure apostolic word there could be no Christian hearing, no word of Christ, no life in the Spirit. It is this issue of the absolute and the relative, the divine and the human, which is behind this problem of order in the relation between the man and the woman.

When the apostle says that "the man is not without the woman nor the woman without the man," he makes it plain that he is not retracting anything said in the epistle to the Galatians about there being no male and female in Christ (3:28). On the other hand, only an unattentive enthusiasm could arrive, from what he had said there, at the conclusion

32. Barth, *K.D.*, III/1, p. 355 [310].

that the man is *as* the woman and the woman *as* the man, as though there were no question of super- and subordination between them. God is a God of order; and peace can be maintained in the church only if this order, with the distinction it implies, is observed.

For Barth, then, the whole argument in I Corinthians 11 turns to verse 3b, the affirmation that "the man is the head of the woman." And what is the basis of this affirmation? Here reference might be made, says Barth, to Ephesians 5:22-23, where it is explained that the man is the head of the woman as Christ also is the head of the church. The whole point of the statement in the Ephesians passage is that the man, in his relationship to the woman, represents Christ in his relationship to the church. However, even apart from the Ephesians statement it is clear that the observance of the right relationship between the sexes is necessary because the distinctions of the relative, indirect, human order (the man is the "head" of the woman) rest on those of the absolute, direct, divine order (the "head" of every man is Christ). This, says Barth, is the connection between the divine work of salvation and the order of human relationships.

It should be noted, of course, that in I Corinthians 11 Paul does not arrange his affirmations so as to move up or down a scale. He does not say that God is the head of Christ, who is the head of the man, who is the head of the woman. The apostle, Barth admits, has often been interpreted in this way, with the absurd consequence that the man is to the woman what Christ is to the man. But the remarkable sequence that Paul follows warns us against this interpretation. The statement that the man is set above the woman is preceded by the statement that Christ is set above the man. And this same statement that subordinates the woman to the man is followed by the statement that Christ is subordinate to God (I Cor. 11:3). Thus both the superordination of the man and the subordination of the woman are principally and properly in Christ, who is the head of all rule and authority (Col. 2:10), in whom all things are summed up (Eph. 1:10), to whom all authority is given in heaven and on earth (Mt. 28:18).

Whatever authority, therefore, may be given to the man in relation to the woman, it is legitimate and effective only to the extent that he merely attests and represents the authority which primarily and properly belongs not to him but to Christ. Conversely, Christ humbled himself in complete obedience ("He was made sin for us," II Cor. 5:21 — who could stoop lower than that!) that by becoming the servant of God and Man he might be exalted. Christ, then, sums up all subordination. As he stands higher than the man, so he stands lower than the woman. Hence, whatever authority the woman may lack in her relationship to the man, the relationship she sustains to the man is sanctified, ennobled, and glorified by the fact that the woman attests and represents the submission which primarily and properly belongs not to her but to Christ. Thus the affirmation, "the head of the woman is the man," is said between the height of Christ's lordship and the depth of his humiliation.

Thus it is little indeed, says Barth, that this statement ascribes to the man or denies to the woman, so sharply and clearly is it determined and limited on both sides by what is properly the matter of Christ. His is the superordination and the subordination; his is the place of both the man and the woman. Yet it is no little thing for the man to be the head of the woman, i.e. to take the precedence, initiative, and authority, as representative of the order which embraces them both. And it is no little thing for the woman to take the place assigned to her in relation to the man and therefore to accept his authority, to be led by him and to recognize the order which claims them both. This basic order, established by the Creator in the realm of the human, is not accidental or contingent, because it is grounded in Christ with a view to whom heaven and earth and man himself were created.

But, continues Barth, since in Christ all things are created new, Galatians 3:28 is still true. This is so in spite of a so-called contradiction which some exegetes, like the short-sighted Corinthians themselves, claim to see between this text in Galatians and I Corinthians 11. The mutuality of the man/woman relationship, then, exists, but it exists in the way in which it is described in I Corinthians 11. And to this extent, also, there is an equality of the man and the woman in the Lord, who has assigned to the man *this* place and to the woman *that* place, even in the church. Here is where there is a real knowledge both of mutuality and of differentiation.

Where but in the church of Christ, Barth asks, is the oppression of the woman radically excluded? And in Ephesians 5, is not the church itself adduced as the model of the woman who finds her head in the man and cannot really exist except in subordination to the head in whom she is exalted? Hence the order established in creation cannot be broken in the church, nor can it imperil either the man or the woman in their self-fulfillment under God.

And so there is no cause to abolish this order as a mere convention, for it is no mere convention. Progress beyond this convention could only be regress to the old aeon. Only in the world of the old aeon could the "feminist question" arise. For this reason, in Corinth the custom in question (wearing veils) had to be allowed to stand. It was symbolic recognition of the relationship as it has been given in Christ. While it might have taken another form in another age, in Corinth it was called in question in this form and therefore had to be defended in this form for the sake of what was at issue in this form.[33]

Barth concludes his discussion of the male/female hierarchy in *Dogmatik*, III/2, by giving considerable attention to Ephesians 5:22-23, a passage which he styles the *locus classicus* of the point at issue. In this Scripture, it will be recalled, the apostle admonishes husbands to love their wives as Christ loved the church, and wives to reverence (the Greek is φοβέω, "to fear") their husbands. No other passage, says Barth, is so emphatic and so primarily concerned to expound the two relationships, the one between the man and the woman (husband and wife) and the other between Christ and the church, as the latter reflects the former and the former is grounded in the latter.

From the vantage point of this Scripture we can survey the whole landscape of the question. This passage sums up the New Testament doctrine of the relationship between Christ and the church; and it does so in terms of the relationship between man and woman. This doctrine, set forth in Ephesians 5, corresponds to the Old Testament understanding of the relationship of man and woman reflected in the Song of Songs. This understanding, in turn, is derived from the relationship of Jahweh to Israel. And the final starting-point of all is

33. Barth, *K.D.*, III/2, p. 376 [312].

Genesis 2, where the natural being of Man is understood as a fellowship, a being-in-the-encounter-of-I-and-thou, that is, of the man and the woman, as the image of God. This is why Ephesians 5 is the passage that finally makes everything clear.

Now chapter 5 of Ephesians is the introduction to the so-called Ephesian *Haustafel*,[34] a list of specific admonitions to wives, husbands, children, parents, slaves and masters, as members of the Christian community. All these admonitions, Barth reminds us, stand under the overruling injunction: "Be filled with the Spirit . . . submitting yourselves to one another in the fear of Christ" (vv. 18, 21). In the fellowship of the gospel, therefore, it is not might that gives one his right(s), but a reciprocal subordination in which each gives the other his proper due. This is the meaning of the "house-table" in Ephesians. Here, then, is no patriarchalism, no hierarchical control of the one over the other, no dominion on the part of one over the other. The submission in verse 21 is reciprocal; it applies equally to all, each in his own place and in his own way.

The advantage of the wife is that the particular admonition addressed to her is a form of the basic admonition addressed to all. She is in subordination to her husband as is the whole Christian community to Christ. And the husband must take the same position in relation to Christ as does the woman in relation to her husband. That is what makes the admonition to the wife so urgent and inescapable and gives her her peculiar distinction. Thus the wife is not less but greater than her husband in the Christian community; not second but first, since the husband has no option but to order himself after the example of his wife, in the church, as she is subordinate in this way. Strikingly, the whole passage ends by repeating the admonition to the wife that she fear (reverence) her husband (v. 33b).

What is said to the husband in this passage, then, is said in the framework of this initial and concluding admonition to the wife. She is the type of the church listening in submission to Christ. The attitude of the husband, therefore, who in his relationship to his wife is the head, the first, the leader, the superior, the bearer of primary responsibility, finds its meaning

---

34. A term first used in Luther's *Catechism*, meaning literally "house-table," a table of rules for the Christian household, and referring to Eph. 5:22f., Col. 3:18f., Tit. 2:5f., I Pet. 2:18f.

in a mutual subordination in the fear of Christ which is expected of all (v. 21). In this respect he is the type of the Head, of the Author and Lord of the church, the Savior of the body, who submitted to death for our salvation.

Of course, the church must reflect the fact that it is the body of this true Head; for how could it be the body of this Head without this reflection at the human level? Naturally, however, it is only a reflection. Men are not the lords and saviors of women any more than they are the lords and saviors of themselves. Christ stands equally above husbands and wives, even as he stands below them. But the reflection of his majesty and lowliness in relation to them is the particular responsibility of husbands in relation to their wives. They must love their wives as Christ loved the church. Thus Christ-and-the-church is the basic decree, the plan of all God's plans, the normative pattern for the creation of Man; and Man's creation climaxes with humanity in the form of man and woman. This is the "great mystery" of Ephesians 5:32.[35]

For one last time Barth takes up the theme of man and woman in Dogmatik, III/4. In this final statement he gives special attention to the Greek verb used to describe the woman's relationship to the man, ὑποτάσσεσθαι, meaning literally, "to stand under," and translated, "to submit to," "to be in subjection to," "to be subject to," "to keep one's place." Such an expression occurs no fewer than seven times in the New Testament when speaking of the woman's relationship to the man (I Cor. 14:34; Eph. 5:22, 24; Col. 3:18; I Tim. 2:11; Titus 2:5; I Pet. 3:1). What do these admonitions require of the woman in relation to the man, and specifically of the wife in relation to her husband?

Barth tells us that the right answer depends on the correct translation of the Greek original. "In no sense" is the meaning to be conceived in terms of the relationship of owner and chat-

35. The above is a summary of Barth's argument for woman's subordination as found in K.D., III/2, pp. 372-381 [309-316]. Here it must be remembered that Barth assumes that the man/woman relationship in general is illumined by the husband/wife relationship in particular. Though he recognizes the "decentralization" of marriage with the advent of the Messiah, yet Ephesians 5 is the key to the meaning of Genesis 2 because Christ and the church (the spiritual husband and wife) are the final meaning of everything, including the creation, especially the creation of Man as male and female.

tel, of superior and subordinate, or even of prince and subject.[36] The term, to be sure, speaks of sequence and subordination, but in such a way that the emphasis lies on a proper order in the relationship of the woman to the man. It is a matter of mutual adaptation and coordination. The authority to which the woman bows in her subordination to the man is not that of the man as such, but the τάξις (order) under which they both are placed. (It is not too much to say, avers Barth, that the man in his place, in that he is obedient to the same Lord who imposes this same τάξις [order] on him, thereby subordinates himself to the woman.) The subordination of the woman, then, is primarily and essentially to the Lord, only secondarily and unessentially (*sekundär und uneigentlich*) to the man. The relation of the woman to the man is only a special form of the obedience which the church owes to Jesus Christ. Hence it is, at the human level, a mode of subordination which is *sui generis*; it is free, honorable and meaningful, taking nothing from the woman and giving nothing to the man.

Yet there is a real subordination, affirms Barth; there can be no avoiding this fact. The chief statement of Paul on this matter (I Cor. 11) is quite unambiguous. There is an express, irreversible order in the man/woman relationship. Whatever the exact meaning of the word "head" (κεφαλή) may be, if the man is the "head" of the woman, this is decisive for the fact that the obedience to the ordinance required of both implies his precedence and superordination, her following and subordination. Just how this principle is to be worked out must be decided concretely in the various contexts of life together. The divine command, then, requires that we maintain the ordinance unchanged. But the application of the ordinance changes with time and place. Hence, also, the conduct required or forbidden

---

36. Here see Rom. 13:1 where ὑποτάσσεσθαι is used: "Let every soul be subject to the higher power." Barth is arguing that Eph. 5:22, and similar passages, are *not* to be interpreted in the light of Rom. 13:1f. The woman is not *under* the man as the subject is *under* the prince, even though Paul uses the same verb in both instances. Interestingly, Emil Brunner rejects the "head-of-the-house" view of the husband's role as Old Testament patriarchalism; yet at the same time he speaks, using quotation marks, of the man's "political" leadership in the home and of the "monarchy" of the family (*Das Gebot und die Ordnungen*; Tübingen: J. C. B. Mohr [Paul Siebeck], 1933, pp. 364-365). This seems to mean that while the woman is not under the man as a subject is under a prince, yet she is under the man as a "subject" is under a "prince."

by the commandment changes with time and place. Yet by the commandment we distinguish obedience to the ordinance from disobedience, whatever the time and place.

In speaking of the various circumstances in which the commandment is given, Barth assumes, of course, that the woman's use of a veil and long hair is a matter of custom. It would be foolish, he affirms, to try to make an inflexible rule out of Paul's statements at this point. The commandment, because it is a living commandment of the living Lord, may indeed allow a woman of today to lay aside a veil, to cut her hair, and to break her silence in the sacred assembly. But the important point in I Corinthians 11 and 14 is not the historical context of Paul's day, out of which he spoke, but the upholding of the eternal commandment in our day, a commandment which for all eternity directs the man and the woman to their proper place and forbids all attempts to violate the ordinance which governs the relationship of the sexes.[37]

And so we conclude our survey of Barth's teaching concerning sexual hierarchy. That the woman, in all things, is subordinate to the man is the conclusion drawn from three fundamental postulates about Man as male and female. These three postulates, which constitute the essence of Barth's theology of sexuality, may be summarized as follows:

First: Man, as created, stands before God in the either/or of male and female being. One is required, therefore, genuinely and fully to accept one's sex, seeking neither to deny it nor to transcend it.

Second: Man, as created male or female, is so created that relationship to one's sexual partner is fundamental to all of life. There is no such thing as self-sufficient male life or female life. "The man is not without the woman nor the woman without the man." Hence Man is male and female.

Third: Man, created as male and female, is related to his sexual partner by a definite order of preceding and following, of super- and subordination. The man is superordinate to the woman; the woman, subordinate to the man. This is that aspect of the whole question which Barth calls "the most

37. The above summary is based on *K.D.*, III/4, pp. 192-196 [172-176].

delicate," *et pour cause*. Consequently, in the defense of this last thesis, he has expended no ordinary effort.[38]

4. An Evaluation

F. W. Grosheide, commenting on I Corinthians 11, observes that this Scripture postulates "a difference which puts the man *above* the woman, a difference we should never forget, since it is an ordinance of creation." Yet, he continues,

> . . . though the woman is given a place below the man, verse eleven ["the woman is not without the man nor the man without the woman, in the Lord"] makes abundantly clear that she is not the slave of the man. Her inferior position is not because man has a greater degree of dignity than she. On the contrary the apostle Paul fights on two fronts. On the one side it was necessary to put the emancipated Corinthian ladies in their places, but on the other Paul seeks to prevent the woman from being considered inferior.[39]

One may or may not be persuaded of a sexual hierarchy whereby the woman is subordinate to the man, but in any case one can hardly escape the impression that Barth is "fighting on two fronts," as Grosheide remarks of Paul. As a result the argument in his hands dies of a thousand qualifications. The woman is subordinate "in this respect," "from this standpoint," and "to this extent." But it is not easy to determine in *what* respect, from *what* standpoint and to *what* extent her subordination is to be understood.

The woman is subordinate to the man in such a way that the man subordinates himself to the woman; her subordination is real, express, irreversible; yet it is not like any other instance of subordination. It is not like subordination to one's superior,

---

38. What is difficult for Barth is easy for some. See, for example, C. Peter Wagner, *A Turned-On Church in an Uptight World* (Grand Rapids: Zondervan, 1971), ch. 7, "Woman and Wine," the section, "First Difficulty: Women," pp. 78f.

39. F. W. Grosheide, *Commentary on the First Epistle to the Corinthians*, in *The New International Commentary on the New Testament*, ed. F. F. Bruce (Grand Rapids: Eerdmans, 1953), p. 258. One might wonder how one can speak of "emancipated ladies" being "put in their places," as Grosheide does in this place, without implying what he is so careful to deny in the next breath, viz., that women are to be considered inferior.

for the man is not superior; not like the subordination of the
believer to Christ, for the man is not the savior of the woman
any more than she is the savior of the man; not like the subordination of subject to prince, though the apostle uses the same
word, ὑποτάσσεσθαι, in both Romans 13:1 and Ephesians 5:24.
The man's preeminence is such as involves his humiliation; the
wife's relation to her husband is such that she is really greater
than he, not second but first; the headship of the man as leader
finds its meaning in the mutual subordination expected of all
who are in Christ. The authority to which the woman submits
is not that of the man, but of the "order" under which they
both are placed. This order of super- and subordination calls
for a "reciprocal subordination" in which each gives the other
his proper due.

One is reminded of Capulet's protestations to his daughter,
Juliet, when she tried to tell him that she was his grateful and
thankful child, but did not intend to marry the man he had
chosen for her:

How now, how now, chop-logic! What is this?
"Proud", and "I thank you", and "I thank you not";
And yet "not proud": mistress minion, you,
Thank me no thankings, nor proud me no prouds,
But fettle your fine joints 'gainst Thursday next,
To go with Paris to Saint Peter's Church,
Or I will drag thee on a hurdle thither.[40]

Reminding us of the fact that the man/woman relationship involves a definite order which must not be confused, reversed, or interchanged but only faithfully maintained, Barth
says over and over again that man and woman are different,
not an A and a second A, like two halves of an hourglass, but
an A and a B. A has not the slightest advantage over B, nor
B over A. Man and woman are fully equal before God and
therefore in their human existence fully equal also. Yet A is
not B but A, and B is not A but B.

This sort of reasoning cannot be faulted; but so far as the
question before us is concerned, it does not seem to advance
anywhere, it does not move toward any resolution of the issue.
The difference of the woman from the man is beyond dispute.
The issue is: Does this difference imply subordination? Can

40. Shakespeare, Romeo and Juliet, Act III, scene v, ll. 150ff.

Barth (or anyone else) establish the mooted point — woman's *subordination to* the man — by underscoring the obvious point — woman's *difference from* the man — without the help of the traditional point — woman's *inferiority to* the man? The answer, it appears, is no.

Furthermore, Barth's exegesis of certain crucial passages, especially I Corinthians 11, leaves something to be desired. Is he justified, for example, in making what he does of the sequence of Paul's affirmations in I Corinthians 11:3? What if the affirmation of man's headship over the woman is preceded by that of Christ's headship over the man and followed by that of God's headship over Christ? Does this sequence really bear in any material way on the meaning of the headship of the man over the woman in the apostle's argument? It is hardly evident from Barth's analysis that it does. And while one may, as Barth does, conclude that it would be foolish to make an inflexible rule of Paul's statements about the woman's veil and hair, it is by no means clear that Paul would agree. He speaks of the woman's covered head as something which "nature (φύσις) itself teaches," in distinction from mere custom. A woman's hair is "given her as a covering." Given by whom? By God her Creator. To dismiss this language by making it appear that Paul is thinking only in terms of social proprieties is simply to evade the text. In this passage the apostle reasons in the same way he does in Romans 1:26-27 where he speaks of homosexuality as "against nature (φύσις)," that is, against what nature itself teaches us. This is not to say that he was as shocked with the behavior of the Corinthian women as he was offended with that of homosexuals. But it is to say that he regarded both kinds of behavior as contrary to the will of God as that will confronts us in the ordinances of creation.

In Ephesians 5:22-24, the apostle describes the woman's relation to the man by the verb "to stand under"(ὑποτάσσεσθαι). Barth seeks to explain this relationship in terms of proper order and sequence, of natural adaptation and coordination, until at last he virtually has the man standing under the woman. How can this be the ultimate meaning of a text which plainly says the reverse? When he gets through explaining how the woman is subordinate to the man, the question is, "Wherein does the subordination consist?" It is a subordination which is honorable, giving nothing, taking nothing, yet somehow reflecting the subordination of the church to Christ. This is, indeed, a subordination which is *sui generis!*

One wonders, in all this, why Barth does not work through to the clear conclusion which follows from his own theology of Man as male and female. Man and woman are partners in life, significantly different from each other but definitely equal to each other; so related to each other as to be a fellowship like God himself; the very image of him who is the Father, the Son, and the Holy Spirit. How then can he escape the conclusion that there is no absolute, invariable *super-* and *sub*ordination between the sexes at the human level?

Here, it seems, is the fundamental difficulty with Barth's argument for female subordination: *the theology of Man as male and female, which he himself has espoused, is inimical to a doctrine of sexual hierarchy. The basic thrust of that theology is rather one of a fellowship of equals under God.* Barth has perceived — correctly, we believe — the implication of the creation ordinance whereby God made Man male and female. So far as the relationship between man and woman is concerned, this implication is one of mutual partnership in life. Yet he draws back from following this implication to the conclusion to which it leads. He seeks to maintain the traditional subordination of the woman to the man without acknowledging the traditional theological grounds on which this subordination is based, namely, the superiority of the man as the image and glory of God in whom the discretion of reason predominates.

Is Barth, then, a male chauvinist after all, albeit an erudite one? We do not think so. But neither can we agree that his argument for sexual hierarchy is convincing. We must, then, gird up the loins of our minds as we review the whole question from a somewhat different perspective. In seeking to gain this new perspective, we shall first review the teaching of the Old Testament and Judaism concerning women. Here we shall see how the view implied in the original creation narratives, that the man and the woman are partners in the fellowship of life, was largely lost sight of because the culture of Israel, God's ancient people, was so completely patriarchal. In all patriarchal societies, Israel being no exception, the man rules over the woman; she is not in partnership with him, but sub-

ordinate to him as his inferior. Then we shall turn to a consideration of Jesus' view of women. In his public ministry a
new thing happened: he spoke of women and related to women
as being fully human and equal in every way to men. In this
respect Jesus was truly a revolutionary. Though he was born
and lived in a culture that assumed the inferiority of the
woman and her subordination to the man, he himself broke
radically with that assumption, thus restoring to the woman
the full humanity which was given her by the Creator when
he made Man male and female.

When one compares and contrasts the patriarchalism
found in the Old Testament with the teaching of Jesus about
women, one becomes aware of a dialectic in Scripture itself.
This dialectic in Scripture — and in Barth's theology — is
focused most sharply in Paul, the former rabbi who became
the apostle of Christian liberty. It was he who spoke the most
decisive word both in favor of woman's subjection (I Cor. 11)
and in favor of woman's liberation (Gal. 3).

We must, then, give special attention to Paul, whose teaching constitutes a kind of *crux interpretum*. Having revisited the
Pauline argument for female subordination, we shall look once
more at the second creation narrative and seek to come to a
firm conclusion as to what it means to say that the woman was
created *from* and *for* the man. When we have done this, the
dialectic of Scripture to which we have referred will be seen for
what it is. And this insight, in turn, will indicate the direction
in which our thought will proceed as we seek a resolution to
the question: What is the Christian view of the man/woman
relationship?

D. *Women in the Old Testament and in Judaism*

In ancient Israel women shared with men in the grace of
God as members of the covenant community; they participated
in the cultic life of the people and, in exceptional cases, even
assumed a prominent role of leadership. While the term
"prophetess" may, at times, have been an honorary title given
the wife of a prophet (Is. 8:3), at other times it clearly refers
to women who exercised the prophetic gift, as Miriam in the

days of Moses (Ex. 15:20), Deborah in the time of the Judges
(Jdg. 4:4), and Huldah during the reign of Josiah (II Kgs.
22:14). Women in Israel, especially in earlier times, associated
freely with men, as did Rebekah and the maidens who came
to the well outside the city to draw water (Gen. 24:10f.),
and Ruth, the Moabitess, who gleaned with the women in the
fields of Boaz (Ruth 2:2ff.). The law allowed that a daughter
might inherit the possession of her father if he died without a
male heir (Nu. 27:1f.), though such a woman had to marry in
her own tribe in order to retain the inheritance (Nu. 36).

All in all, however, women lived in the shadows rather
than in the light of life in Old Testament Israel. It was a man's
world. In the Scriptures of the Old Testament many things
are reported about the treatment of women which would
corroborate the remark of Winternitz: "Woman has always
been the best friend religion ever had; but religion has by no
means been the best friend woman ever had."[41] The cultural
milieu of God's ancient people was patriarchal, which meant
that the men ruled, the women obeyed, in all the major
decisions of life.

A daughter remained under the authority of her father
till she came under the authority of the man to whom she was
given in marriage. She might indeed on occasion be asked to
give her consent to a proposal, as in the case of Rebekah (Gen.
24:58); but the right to give her to a man remained with her
father. His was the freedom to choose, not hers, even though
it was her body, indeed her very self, that was given, and sometimes the parental choice was most arbitrary and unworthy.
Saul, for example, gave his elder daughter Michal to David
"that she might be a snare for him" (I Sam. 18:17ff.). Un-
successful in this stratagem, he took her from David and gave
her to Palti, son of Laish (I Sam. 25:44). Her later restoration
to David was marked by trauma (II Sam. 3:13) and mistrust
(II Sam. 6:16f.).

It was the custom of the groom to pay for the bride with
money, animals, and even work. Suffused with love, this custom
could be ennobled, as when Jacob worked seven years for

41. As quoted by A. Schimmel, "Frau," "Religionsgeschichtlich," *Die Religion in Geschichte und Gegenwart* (Tübingen: J. C. B. Mohr [Paul Sie-
beck], 1958), II, p. 1066.

Rachel's hand (Gen. 29:18-20), but it tended to reduce the woman to an object that could be bought; she became the possession of the man.[42] If, when a man had taken a woman to wife, he found "some indecency"[43] in her, he had only to give her a bill of divorce and thrust her out of his house (Deut. 24:1). No one dreamed of giving the woman a similar right, though her husband might be guilty of much more than an "indecency." Viewed from an historical standpoint, such a law protected the woman from an even more arbitrary act of repudiation, but it obviously falls far below the Christian ideal of justice.

While under the authority of a husband, strict fidelity was required of the woman. If a man so much as suspected his wife's integrity ("if the spirit of jealousy came upon him"), by an ancient rite she could be made to drink the "water of bitterness that brings the curse." If guilty, she had to "bear her iniquity"; if innocent, she was free from the curse. But in any case "the man shall be free from iniquity" (Nu. 5:11-31). Presumably the man who is declared without iniquity in this case (v. 31) is the accusing husband. But why should a woman, even if she were guilty, drink alone the bitter water for a sin she could not possibly have committed alone?

When married, if the wife did not present her husband with a son, such reproach was cast upon her that she would sometimes have recourse to doubtful expedients. A woman of means who possessed slave girls would use them to relieve her distress, thus contributing to the degradation of her own sex. (See the account of Sarah and Hagar, Gen. 16:1-6, and that of Rachel and Bilhah, Gen. 30:1-13.) Even if she were fortunate enough to have a husband who loved her, a barren wife had a heavy cross to bear. Though her husband did not repudiate her, his other wives knew how to make her miserable as a failure in life. When we read of the devout Hannah, whose

42. In Israel this tendency was happily restrained and the bride might even receive gifts in her own right which became her personal property (Gen. 24:53; 34:12). The Israelites also knew something of the mutuality and reciprocity with which genuine love informs marriage even in a strongly patriarchal culture. The erotic love poems in the Song of Solomon eloquently testify to this fact.

43. Literally, "nakedness of a thing." The Hebrew ערות דבר is obscure, an obscurity exploited by the followers of Hillel in giving the law a broad application favorable to the husband.

"rival used to provoke her sorely" till she "wept and would not eat" (I Sam. 1:3-8), the pathos is relieved by the happy denouement of the story. God heard Hannah's prayer and she became a mother; moreover, the mother of a son; indeed, the mother of one of the great prophets of Israel. But how many women like Hannah must have suffered without relief, adding their tears and sighs to those of the disinherited who, through the centuries, have cried unto the Lord of hosts?

If the husband of a woman died and had no son, his brother was to take her as his wife and raise up seed to his brother. Though the man could refuse such Levirate marriage, the woman could not (Deut. 25:1-10). This freedom of refusal on the man's side worked favorably for the Moabitess Ruth, who thereby became the wife of the devout and affluent Boaz (Ruth 4:1-12). But this happy turn does not alter the fact that the law did not consider the woman to have any freedom of choice in the matter, whereas Christian doctrine says that self-determination is of the essence of the divine image and that the woman shares equally with the man in this endowment. In this regard one should note, in the narrative concerning Ruth, the expression of purchase, as of an object, used twice over: "The day you buy the field . . . you are also *buying* Ruth" (v. 5); "Also Ruth . . . I have *bought* to be my wife . . ." (v. 10).

The Book of the Covenant, which defines the norm of moral conduct for Israel (Ex. 20-23), when compared with similar documents in the ancient Near East, reflects a high sense of the worth of human life as greater than all material values. Yet the Decalogue — an incomparable summation of the duty required of Man — with which this section begins, admonishes one against coveting his neighbor's house, *wife*, slave girl, ox, ass, or any*thing* that belongs to his neighbor. Obviously this list is addressed to the man as head of the house, the one who *possesses* all these things: house, wife, slaves, and animals. Of course this does not mean that in Israel all these things were considered to be of like value. (In Deut. 5:21 the wife is at least mentioned first in stating the tenth commandment.) But it is a mode of expression that shows how far women were from being considered equal to their husbands as persons.[44]

This domination by the male — first by her father, then her husband, then her husband's brother — touched all aspects of the woman's life in Israel. She was a second-class citizen from birth. This fact was symbolically expressed in restricting the initiatory rite of circumcision, which was the sign of the covenant, to males (Gen. 12). Though the woman was a member of the covenant community, she never received the sign which marked one for life as enjoying the rights and privileges of such a fellowship.[45]

This symbolic exclusion of the woman from the full status of covenant privilege increasingly became a real exclusion with the lapse of time. Although Hannah received a portion of the yearly sacrifice when she accompanied her husband to Shiloh, and although she enjoyed free access to the house of the Lord in the exercise of prayer (I Sam. 1:3f.), and although the temples later erected at Jerusalem by Solomon and by the exiles returning under Cyrus gave women these same privileges, in the temple built by Herod (4 B.C.) women were excluded from the court of the men. Josephus (Antiquitates) mentions the area designated for women in the temple, using the same word to describe it which the Greeks used for the harem (γυναικωνίτις).

During the time of their monthly purification, and also for a period of forty days after the birth of a son (cf. Lk. 2:22) and eighty days after the birth of a daughter (Lev. 12:2-5), women were not allowed even in the court of the Gentiles.[46] According to the Mishna, the court of the women was not only further removed from the Holy of Holies than was the court of the men, but it was also fifteen steps lower. Likewise in the synagogue, an institution traceable from the third century B.C., women began to be more and more segregated from the men,

44. The fundamental mind-set toward the woman as less a person than the man is reflected in the story — shocking by Christian standards — of Abraham's abandoning Sarah, his wife, to Pharaoh's embrace in order to save his own skin (Gen. 12:10-13:1).

45. Significantly, the corresponding New Testament rite of initiation reflects no such symbolic impediment. Women have always received baptism along with men.

46. Jeremias, Jerusalem in the Time of Jesus, p. 373, with sources. Note the double ceremonial defilement implied in the birth of a female.

especially after the destruction of the temple in A.D. 70.
Eventually synagogues were built so that men and women
would not come into physical contact during worship.[47]

This lack of visibility in a physical sense in the worshipping
community led inevitably to a curtailment of the woman's
participation. Any male member of the congregation might be
asked by the ruler of the synagogue to read the law or the
prophets as occasion required. But to the woman such reading
was forbidden; she must preserve a strict silence. "The woman
does not read out of the Torah for the sake of the honor of the
congregation."[48]

In fact the woman was not even counted as a member of
the congregation. In order for a congregation to exist there
had to be at least ten men; nine men plus all the women in
Israel would not be sufficient. Since the woman, along with
slaves and children, was remanded to silence in worship
(women, slaves and children were frequently bracketed together
in rabbinic thought), it was considered undesirable to give a
girl serious religious instruction. Rabbi Eliezer ben Hyrkanos
pronounced: "He who teaches his daughter the law, teaches
her lechery."[49] Under such circumstances the woman naturally
became the victim of religious aberrations. "Many women, many
superstitions," complained Hillel. Even in her private religious
devotions, the woman was not the equal of the man; her father
or her husband, as the case might be, could nullify her vows
(Nu. 30). The superior wisdom in the man which this law
supposes is hardly confirmed by the vow of Jephthah (Jdg.
11:30).

Concomitantly with this treating of the woman as inferior
in her religious sensibilities, there emerged in Judaism an overt
contempt of the female sex. "Happy is he whose children are
males, and woe to him whose children are females." "Were the
words of the Torah to be burned, they should not be handed
over to women."[50] Women were not to teach anyone — not
even children, according to some authorities — nor recite the

---

47. Jeremias, *Jerusalem in the Time of Jesus*, p. 374.
48. Megilla 23a (Baraitha), as quoted by J. Leipoldt, *Die Frau in der antiken Welt und im Urchristentum*, p. 55. For Paul's views on women keeping silent in the churches, see I Cor. 14:34, 35.
49. Leipoldt, *Die Frau . . .* , p. 56, with sources.
50. For sources see Oepke, "γυνή," *TDNT*, I, p. 781.

Shema. They were not allowed to bear witness, because it was concluded from Genesis 18:15, the passage in which Sarah denied her unbelieving laughter, that women are liars. (Though the Gospels speak of women as the first to encounter the risen Lord, Paul does not mention them when he lists the witnesses to the resurrection in I Cor. 15:5-8.) In contrast to the usage of the honorable title "son of Abraham," that of "daughter of Abraham" is seldom found in rabbinic literature. The adjectives for "pious," "just," and "holy" have no feminine form in Hebrew, an indication of their infrequent application to women.[51] There are warnings not to speak at length with a woman, not even with one's wife. The humorous story is told of a rabbi who asked the wife of a fellow rabbi: "By what route may one go to Lod [Lydda]?" Being a lady of wit, she reminded him of the scholars' dictum against speaking too much with women and suggested that he should have put the question in the shortened form: "What is the way to Lod?"[52]

This desire to restrict the social intercourse of women led to restrictive rules about their appearing in public. In some places, especially the larger cities, women tended to withdraw physically from the outside world. By the same token, when they ventured forth in public, women were to be veiled at least to the extent of having their heads covered. Mother Kimchith (Qimhit) had seven sons, all of whom served as high priests. When asked by the scholars what she had done to attain such success as a mother in Israel, it is reported that she replied: "Never in my life have the rafters of my house looked down on my tresses."[53]

Perhaps the saying which most strikingly epitomizes the rabbinic depreciation of women is that of Rabbi Juda ben Elai (c. A.D. 150): "One must utter three doxologies every day: Praise God that he did not create me a heathen! Praise God that he did not create me a woman! Praise God that he did not create me an illiterate person!" Though this prayer is sel-

51. Leipoldt, *Die Frau* . . . , p. 62. "The masculine gender is attributed by the Hebrews and the Semites generally to whatever is . . . courageous, respected, great, strong, powerful . . . ; the feminine to whatever is motherly, productive, sustaining, nourishing, gentle, weak, . . . subject" (*Gesenius' Hebrew Grammar*, Second English Edition [Oxford: Oxford Univ. Press, 1910], p. 391, note 3).

52. Leipoldt, *Die Frau* . . . , p. 62.

53. Leipoldt, *Die Frau* . . . , pp. 64-65.

dom, if ever, uttered today, one cannot, as Leipoldt observes, minimize its historical significance by regarding it as the jaundiced opinion of an individual misogynist. It appears no less than three times in the older rabbinic literature and was looked upon by Jewish authorities as a normative statement.[54] This prayer, which Rabbi Juda commends, was faithfully offered for centuries in the synagogue, in the hearing of women, who were taught to pray simply: "Praise God that he created me."

To summarize: In the Jewish conception of the relation between man and woman, the man was obviously considered superior as a person, the woman inferior. Therefore the man was to rule, the woman to obey, in all things. Given this inadequate understanding of the meaning of human life as a fellowship of male and female, small wonder that the rabbis came to define the religious ideal in such a way as to exclude the woman from fully sharing it with the man, even with the one man to whom she was most intimately joined, her husband. Though the woman, and only the woman, could utter the blessing at the beginning of the Sabbath, and though she might utter the "amen" when family prayer was offered at mealtime; nonetheless, when her husband purposed to deepen his own understanding of the law, it was necessary for him to withdraw from his wife.[55] The highest exercise of the human spirit, namely, the cultivation of religious devotion, required that the man should separate himself even from the woman who was his wife, since she was incapable of such pursuits.

This thought that one who would give himself in earnest to the study of the law must separate from his wife for a time was expressed so frequently that exact rules were gradually established. The oldest source of these is the *Testament Naphthalis* (8, 8):

> There is a time when man should be together with his wife, and a time when he should keep himself from her for prayer. The rabbis expound thus: He who, by a vow, will renounce his wife, may do so for two weeks in the opinion of the school of Shammai; for one week, according to the school of Hillel. "The pupils [of rabbis], who travel to study

54. Leipoldt, *Die Frau* . . . , pp. 58-59.
55. As for Paul's instructions concerning the separation of husband and wife for religious devotion, see I Cor. 7:5. Here the thought is quite different, since the separation is by a mutual consent, as indeed it ought to be.

the law, may also without [their wiyes'] consent, separate
themselves from them for thirty days, laboring men for one
week" — a stipulation so much more instructive as it is
considered valid not only for those who devote themselves
to the law in a professional way, but for others as well.
This tradition mirrors the over-all Jewish view. The law
stands above all as God's highest gift. He who would
devote himself to it, must be ready to renounce his wife;
she cannot help him, but only be a hindrance to him. But
the obligation to marriage is a part of the law. Therefore
the individual may separate from his wife for a limited
time only.[56]

E. Jesus and Women

Although Jesus sometimes sharply contrasted his own teachings with those of the Jewish leaders of his day, there is no
evidence that he did this when it came to the question of the
woman's place in society. We never read in the Gospels: "It
has been said of old time, women shall not read the law in the
synagogue; but I say unto you, women shall have the same
privileges as men in this regard." Jesus never clashed with the
religious leaders about women's rights as he did about doing
good on the Sabbath day, or praying and giving alms to the
glory of God rather than to be seen of men.

Of course he protested the deliberate exploitation of widows and orphans; those who piously engage in prayer and at
the same time "devour widows' houses" are the object of his
scathing rebuke. But in this he was doing no more than the
reforming prophets before him. It was not so much in what he
said as in how he related to women that Jesus was a revolutionary. In this relationship his life style was so remarkable
that one can only call it astonishing. He treated women as fully
human, equal to men in every respect; no word of deprecation
about women, as such, is ever found on his lips. As the Savior
who identified with the oppressed and the disinherited, he
talked to women and about women with complete freedom and
candor.[57]

56. Leipoldt, Die Frau . . . , p. 79. The rabbinic commentary is from
Kethubboth vi. 6.
57. This appeal to Jesus' life style as "the Savior who identified with the op-

How differently Jesus conceived the relationship between men and women from that which prevailed in ancient Israel can be appreciated by comparing the prohibition he gave his disciples (Mt. 5:28) with the law of Deuteronomy 21:10f. The latter passage declares what a man may do who sees a beautiful woman among the captives of war and desires her as a wife. According to the Deuteronomist he may take her. But should he later tire of her he cannot sell such a woman for money; he must give her her freedom. This was surely an improvement over the common practice of regarding women as simply spoils of war. But Jesus' pronouncement is a radical break with the Deuteronomic regulation. As a strict monogamist, he declared that whosoever as much as looked on a woman to lust after her in his heart was guilty of adultery. In saying this, he attacked head on the double standard of morality which condones in the male a behavior which is condemned in the female.[58]

Speaking of a double standard of morality, it is evident that the men of Israel were no exception to this universal rule in their style of life. When, for example, Judah was told that Tamar, his daughter-in-law, had played the harlot and was with child, his righteous indignation knew no bounds. "Bring her forth and let her be burnt" was his judgment, as swift as it was severe (Gen. 38:24). Only when implicated himself as the man in the case did he mollify these sentiments.

----

pressed and disinherited" indicates the position we take on the deeper question of Christology. There is a temptation to interpret Jesus in terms of the latest "ism," in this case "feminism," a temptation that often betrays the integrity of critical history; yet one must always decide whether Jesus was more than a culturally conditioned first-century Jew. Our treatment of the question of Jesus and women assumes that he was. Hence we are not convinced by statements, like Krister Stendahl's, in his *The Bible and the Role of Women* (Philadelphia: Fortress, 1966), p. 26, that all of Jesus' sayings about the man/ woman relationship fall within the views common to first-century Palestinian Judaism. The revelation of God in Christ is not simply a matter of the *logia* of Jesus. For a perceptive statement in this regard, see C. F. D. Moule, *The Phenomenon of the New Testament* (Naperville, Ill.: Allenson, 1967), pp. 63f.: "Jesus and the Women of the Gospels."

58. The trouble with the double standard is not simply that men have acted by such a rule, but they have even justified it in theory; and it has been a miserable argument indeed. Simone de Beauvoir, noting that prostitution has from antiquity followed the family like a dark shadow, observes: "Sewers are necessary to guarantee the wholesomeness of palaces, according to the Fathers of the Church. And it has often been remarked that the necessity exists of sacrificing one part of the female sex in order to save the other." *The Second Sex*, tr. H. M. Parshley (New York: Knopf, 1953), p. 523.

The men of Jesus' day betrayed much the same prejudice, if one accepts the story found in some of the early copies of John's Gospel.[59] Having seized a woman taken in the act of adultery, they dragged her before Jesus, reminding him of the law that she should be stoned. To be sure, they were not concerned with Jesus' attitude toward women; they were simply using her case to impale him on the horns of a dilemma. Either he must challenge the Roman rulers who alone had the authority to impose the death penalty, or he must set aside the law of Moses. Yet they incidentally betrayed their prejudices in that they laid hold of the woman and not the man; *she* was the sinner who should be a test case. However, the original law to which they appealed said that the woman must be a "virgin betrothed," in which circumstance *both* the man and woman should be stoned (Deut. 22:23f.).

Jesus, in his reply, not only sidestepped the snare which his critics had laid, but cut them down to size with his response: "He who is without sin among you, let him first cast a stone at her" (John 8:3ff.). Of course our Lord did not condone this woman's act. "Go and sin no more" was his earnest admonition to her (John 8:11). But we should not so dwell on his admonition to female folly as to forget his devastating rebuke to male arrogance.[60]

59. Though omitted from the oldest manuscript, the *pericope adulterae* (John 7:53 - 8:11) is thought by some scholars to be an authentic account whose proper location has been lost. The writer personally inclines to this view.

60. Such male arrogance is well illustrated in Boswell's great biography of Dr. Samuel Johnson, the arbiter of eighteenth-century literary usage. "He [Johnson] talked of the heinousness of the crime of adultery, by which the peace of families was destroyed. He said, 'Confusion of progeny constitutes the essence of the crime; and therefore a woman who breaks her marriage vows is much more criminal than a man who does it. A man, to be sure, is criminal in the sight of God; but he does not do his wife a very material injury, if he does not insult her; if, for instance, from mere wantonness of appetite, he steals privately to her chambermaid. Sir, a wife ought not greatly to resent this. I would not receive home a daughter who had run away from her husband on that account. . . . ' Here he discovered that acute discrimination, that solid judgement, and that knowledge of human nature, for which he was upon all occasions remarkable. . . . I asked him if it were not hard that one deviation from chastity should so absolutely ruin a young woman. JOHNSON. 'Why no, Sir; it is the great principle, she has given up every notion of female honor and virtue, which are all included in chastity.' " *Boswell's Life of Johnson*, ed. G. B. Hill (New York: Harper, 1927), I, p. 372.

It cannot be doubted that women in Jesus' presence sensed the difference somehow. Here was a man who violated no proprieties, yet broke through the barriers of tradition and custom in a way that put women completely at ease in his presence. This helps explain the significant fact that, relatively early in his ministry (the Galilean period), mention is made of a group of women disciples who accompanied him on his preaching missions along with the Twelve. Jeremias calls this

> an unprecedented happening in the history of that time. . . . Jesus knowingly overthrew custom when he allowed women to follow him. . . . Jesus was not content with bringing women up onto a higher plane than was the custom; but as Saviour of all, he brings them before God on an equal footing with men.[61]

Among these women followers were Mary Magdalene, out of whom had gone seven demons; Joanna, the wife of Herod's steward; Susanna; and *many* others, Luke tells us. Some of them, it would appear, were women of means "who ministered to him of their substance" (Luke 8:1-3). Jesus' seamless tunic, "woven from the top throughout," a garment so valuable that the soldiers who crucified him cast lots for it (John 19:23, 24), may well have been the gift of one of these affluent women.

These women, some married, some single, who left home and family to follow Jesus throughout the length and breadth of the land, remained faithful even to the end. While of his male disciples one betrayed him, another denied him, and most forsook him, the women, who had followed him all the way from Galilee, were present at the scene of the crucifixion. Among them were Mary Magdalene; Mary the mother of James the Less and of Joses and Salome, who followed Jesus in Galilee and ministered unto him; and many other women who came up with him unto Jerusalem (Mark 15:40, 41).

The detail that they were "beholding from afar" may imply female timidity to those men who look upon courage as a male attribute; but to anyone who knows what a Roman execution was like it will be obvious why the women kept their distance.

61. Jeremias, *Jerusalem in the Time of Jesus*, p. 376.

Some scholars have suggested that even so they risked their lives in what they did.[62] By contrast, according to Matthew 26:56, as soon as Jesus was arrested his male disciples all left him and fled.[63]

Obviously there were many women who were touched deeply by the Master but did not follow him from place to place; family obligations, prevailing custom, and personal considerations prevented them from embarking on such a venture. Yet they too began to awaken to a new self-understanding through contact with him. These women, like all women in Israel, were of little concern to anyone. They went to the synagogue, the central institution in Jewish life, but how could they understand the Scripture and its exposition when all serious instruction in the law was denied them? And since they had nothing to contribute to the understanding of life's basic questions, how could they expect to be taken seriously? But Jesus took them seriously. When they were in his presence the unheard-of happened. He spoke to them in a way that they could understand; he treated them as the real persons they were.

Among such women, two sisters, Mary and Martha, stand out especially. Luke tells us (10:38-42) that when Jesus entered into a certain village a woman named Martha received him, and that she had a sister named Mary who sat at his feet to hear what he had to say. When Martha, unhappy that her sister was not helping her, complained to the Lord, he answered: "Martha, Martha, you are anxious and troubled about many things, but one thing is needful; for Mary has chosen the good part which shall not be taken away from her." Commenting on this passage, Dorothy Sayers observes tersely:

> I think that I have never heard a sermon preached on the story of Martha and Mary that did not attempt, somehow, to explain away its text. Mary's, of course, was the better part — the Lord said so, and we must not precisely contradict him. But we will be careful not to despise Martha. No doubt, he approved of her too. We could not get on

62. Leipoldt, *Die Frau . . .* , p. 86.
63. Harriet Tubman, an escaped slave, made nineteen trips into the South and brought out 300 fellow slaves without loss or capture. It is amusing that slaveholders pledged a large sum for "*him*" dead or alive. Since no *female* was capable of such daring and courage, the name "Harriet" was considered to be an alias.

without her, and indeed (having paid lip service to God's opinion) we must admit that we greatly prefer her. For Martha was doing a really feminine job, whereas Mary was behaving just like any other disciple, male or female; and that is a hard pill to swallow.[64]

If ministers today have trouble accepting the implication of this text, how much more the rabbis of Jesus' day! What Jesus did in this case must have been absolutely incomprehensible to them. They would never dream of entering a house occupied by two unmarried women, let alone discoursing with them, especially concerning spiritual things. Jesus is here showing an utter disregard for custom in order that he might do his kingdom work. And so he fellowshipped with these women who were his disciples even as he fellowshipped with men who were his disciples. He showed the same intimacy and esteem toward Mary and Martha as he showed toward men.

John, generally identified with the "disciple whom Jesus loved" (John 19:26; 20:2; 21:7), tells us that "Jesus loved Martha and her sister and Lazarus" (John 11:5). Thus John's Gospel gives ultimate depth to the relationship between the Master and these two women disciples. According to John 12:1-8, Jesus visited the home of Mary and Martha and Lazarus barely a week before his death. Again the scene is altogether remarkable, though not essentially different from the earlier report of Luke. Martha is serving the meal. The unusual thing is that she is serving a table of men, for not only her brother Lazarus but Judas and evidently Jesus' other disciples were there. In this she assumes a role and performs a service that custom would have allowed only to a man, whether a free servant or a slave.

Her sister Mary goes even further. She does something that only a male, and a slave at that, would have done; she anoints Jesus' feet and wipes them with her hair. To the "unliberated" first-century Jewess, this last touch would have been especially painful. For a woman to take down her hair in the presence of men would have been deemed highly immodest. That a woman could feel such freedom in Jesus' presence must have

64. Dorothy Sayers, Are Women Human? (Grand Rapids: Eerdmans, 1971), p. 46. The observation that the term "disciple" ($\mu\alpha\theta\eta\tau\dot{\eta}\varsigma$) is never used in the Gospels of Jesus' women followers specifically is so much pedanticism. Since they possess the qualifications they are entitled to the name, as our author here assumes.

offended and baffled the men who witnessed it. Judas censured
her gesture as a sentimental extravagance and waste. "Why was
this ointment not sold for three hundred denarii and given to
the poor?" he asked. Jesus rose to Mary's defense, implying that
she had far more awareness of the moment and what was appropriate to it than those who reclined with him at table.
"Leave her alone," was his devastating reply, "that she may
keep the same unto the day of my burial" (v. 7).

Mary, it would seem, was not the first woman thus to
express her love for Jesus. Early in his ministry, while still in
Galilee, he was invited to dine at the home of a Pharisee named
Simon (Lu. 7:36-50). While he reclined at dinner, an unnamed woman entered and, bending over his feet, began to
weep.[65] As she wiped his feet with her hair, she anointed them
with myrrh from a little flask and kissed them in sincere affec-
tion. Tradition has identified this woman as Mary Magdalene.
(This woman was a "sinner" and, after all, what other "demons" could have been exorcised from Mary than those of the
scarlet woman?) But such a reconstruction of history is more a
testimony to male prejudice than a clue to the woman's true
identity.

The cloak of anonymity with which the historian conceals
her from overweening curiosity is in keeping with the paucity
of information he furnishes about the details of her life. She was
evidently a prostitute who had been redeemed through the
ministry of Jesus, perhaps the first man who had ever treated
her as a person rather than a sex object. Her tears probably
expressed not so much her penitence in suing for forgiveness
as her gratitude in sensing that she had received it, though the
Lord then acquitted her, as it were publicly, much to the dis-
pleasure of his fellow guests. Simon his host came off especially
poorly. He assumed he knew more about the woman than
Jesus did, whereas in truth he knew less. He therefore belittled
Jesus for not acting according to his own mean standards, fail-
ing to perceive that the Lord was too noble to be bound by them.
"Simon, do you see this woman?" Jesus asked (v. 44). The un-

---

65. At such meals the guests first removed their sandals and reclined with
their feet behind them. The subsequent intrusion of the uninvited was not
uncommon.

spoken answer was, "No." Having dismissed her as a "sinner," Simon could not see her as a person.

It is not only the intimacy and openness of Jesus' relationship to women that was so significant (and offensive to his contemporaries) but also the social breadth of that relationship. Women came to him from all classes and stations of life. His reputation among women seems to have reached to the highest ranks, for the wife of the governor, no less, sent an earnest message to her husband during Jesus' trial: "Have nothing to do with that just man, for I have suffered this day many things on account of him in a dream" (Mt. 27:19).[66] Some of the women around Jesus, as we have seen, were from the upper class, like Joanna, wife of Herod's steward (Lu. 8:3); some from the lowest class, like the unnamed sinner in a village of Galilee (Lu. 7:37).

The most celebrated instance of his speaking to a woman who was in the wrong class altogether is recorded in John 4. This woman was not only a *woman*, not only a *sinful* woman, but a sinful *Samaritan* woman. Some Jews would not even travel through Samaria, let alone fraternize with the despised half-breeds that lived there. Hence one can understand that when Jesus asked this woman for a drink of water she was more surprised than anyone. "How is it," she asked, "that you, being a Jew, ask a drink of me, being a woman of Samaria?" (v. 7). And when his disciples returned they were simply amazed, though their reverence for him subdued their curiosity (v. 27). Here, as perhaps nowhere else, we see that Jesus conceived the commandment to love one's neighbor as knowing no boundaries of the sort that prejudice erects.

Jesus once praised a poor widow for giving more than the rich (Mk. 12:41f.; Lu. 21:1f.). He commended an importunate mother for her faith, a Syro-Phoenician alien at that (Mt. 15:28). He was always ready to heal women in need, such as Peter's mother-in-law afflicted with fever (Mk. 1:30, 31); the infirm

66. Ernest Renan handles this detail in a way that reflects a shoddy male chauvinism: Jesus, the *beau jeune homme*, had, it seems, a way with women. Even the wife of Pilate, proud Roman lady that she was, when she glimpsed him from her window, became enchanted, dreamed of him at night, and showed alarm at the prospect of his death. *Vie de Jesus*, ch. XXIV, p. 403, as cited in Philip Schaff, *History of the Christian Church* (Grand Rapids: Eerdmans, 1955), I, p. 170.

woman bent over for eighteen years, whom he called a "daughter of Abraham" (Lu. 13:10f.); and the desperate woman with an issue who had suffered many things at the hands of physicians, yet was no better for it, but worse (Mk. 5:25f.). This last case has a peculiar poignancy since the woman had been ritually unclean (Lev. 15:19f.) for twelve years. Thus she was debarred from all cultic activity and rendered unclean anyone she touched. An inevitable sense of degradation and contagion made her shy away from disclosing her "feminine weakness" publicly, as she must needs do were she to ask Jesus for help. Yet she was moved by an unshakable conviction that he could help her. Hence her desperate expedient. She pressed forward till she could touch his garment. Immediately she knew in her body that she was healed. When, in response to Jesus' question, "Who touched me?" she disclosed her secret, so far was he from any concern that he had been touched by one who was unclean that he commended her for her faith and bade her depart in peace.

One of the most distinctive marks of Jesus' teaching method was his use of the parable. The parabolic form was not new; the rabbis had used it. But Jesus' parables are notably different from theirs in that he enriches them with materials drawn from the everyday world of a woman's cares and joys. In them he refers to a woman putting leaven in her meal (Mt. 13:33); to maidens going forth to meet the bridegroom (Mt. 25:1); to an importunate widow who constrained a callous judge to render justice (Lu. 18:1ff.); to a lowly housewife who swept her whole house till she found a lost coin (Lu. 15:8). In this last instance the woman stands for God himself, a matter which bears directly upon the time-honored (but hardly honorable) argument that since God is masculine, only men may represent him in the office of the Christian ministry.

Little wonder, in the light of all these things, that a great multitude of women followed Jesus along the *via dolorosa*, lamenting and mourning him (Lu. 23:27). And Jesus showed himself mindful of their place in his life. Even in this hour of his deepest distress he had a pastoral word for them: "Daughters of Jerusalem, weep not for me . . ." (Lu. 23:28). Some of these faithful women, who followed him to the cross — Mary Magdalene, Mary the mother of James and Salome (Mk. 16:1)—

were the first to whom the Lord appeared after he rose from the dead (Mt. 28:9, 10; cf. Mk. 16:9-11; Jo. 20:11-18). His male disciples first proclaimed the resurrection to the world; but his female disciples first received the revelation on which this proclamation was based.[67] Observing that women were the last at the cross and first at the tomb, Dorothy Sayers gives the reason:

> They had never known a man like this Man — there never has been such another. A prophet and teacher who never nagged at them, never flattered or coaxed or patronized; who never made arch jokes about them, never treated them either as "The women, God help us!" or "The ladies, God bless them"; who rebuked without querulousness and praised without condescension; who took their questions and arguments seriously; who never mapped out their sphere for them, never urged them to be feminine or jeered at them for being female; who had no axe to grind and no uneasy male dignity to defend; who took them as he found them and was completely unselfconscious. There is no act, no sermon, no parable in the whole Gospel that borrows its pungency from female perversity; nobody could possibly guess from the words and deeds of Jesus that there was anything "funny" about woman's nature.[68]

First Addendum:
Concerning "Female Uncleanness"

The Old Testament laws of ritual uncleanness (Lev. 11-16) can hardly be understood in terms of an ultimate dualism in which the soul, pure in essence, is tainted by contact with a body belonging to the material world. Matter is not *per se* evil, for the material world is God's handiwork and therefore a part of God's creation, according to Genesis (see Gen. 1:31). Neither can one say that these laws are purely hygienic, as has been supposed by certain Christian sects who now observe them.

67. In view of the central place that witness to the resurrection had in the early *kerygma* of the apostles (Acts 2:22, 32), the appearance of the risen Lord first to women with the command to tell his brethren (Mt. 28:9-10) is a fact too long overlooked in adjudicating the place of women in the Christian ministry.
68. Dorothy Sayers, *Are Women Human?*, p. 47.

Rather, they seem to have been intended, at the cultic level, to secure the purity of the holy covenant community against the defilement of a ubiquitous paganism.[69]

Jesus respected these ritual laws (Mk. 1:44), yet placed the emphasis on purity of heart, the inward grace corresponding to the outward religious form. In fact, he expressly declared that dietary laws were indifferent (Mk. 7:14-23, par.), a liberating counsel which his disciples were slow to appreciate (Acts 10:15; 11:9. It was Paul who first clearly understood that to the Christian nothing is impure, Rom. 14:14). Jesus' convictions about the ritual impurity accruing to menstruation must have been similar to those he held concerning clean and unclean foods, for he did not tell the woman healed of an issue of blood (Mk. 5:25f.) to show herself to a priest and "offer the things for her purification commanded by Moses." Nor did he regard her touch as defiling so far as his own person was concerned.[70]

This attitude of our Lord respecting menstrual uncleanness is in such contrast to the patristic and medieval canons of the church that one can only marvel at the masculine prejudice reflected in the latter. These canons forbid a woman to approach too near the altar or to receive the sacrament with uncovered hands when she is polluted by her menstrual flow. Gregory I had to assure Augustine of Canterbury that it was not improper for a menstruating woman to enter church and receive Holy Communion, though he commends the reverence of a woman in such condition who abstains.[71] Such an attitude is obviously a regression from the liberty of the gospel to the

69. See the article, "Pur," in Vocabulaire du Théologie Biblique, ed. Xavier Leon-Dufour (Paris: Cerf, 1962).

70. Mark inserts this episode into the account of the raising of Jairus' daughter, whom Jesus "took by the hand" (5:41). The latter is the only recorded instance of his touching a corpse, an act rendering one unclean. In both instances women are involved, a detail which is perhaps not without significance.

71. For sources, with discussion, see Sherwin Bailey, Sexual Relation. . . , p. 47, and his "Women and the Church's Lay Ministry," The Expository Times, 70 (1960), p. 328. As late as 1878, according to Simone de Beauvoir, the British Medical Journal said: "It is an undoubted fact that meat spoils when touched by menstruating women." At the beginning of this century a rule in Northern France forbade women having "the curse" to enter refineries since it would cause the sugar to blacken (The Second Sex, p. 138).

legalism which Paul censured in Galatians, and a male regression at that. This is evident since the Levitical code which
regards a menstruating woman as unclean also pronounces a
man unclean who has an emission of semen. A man who has
intercourse with a woman during her menstrual flow is equally
unclean (Lev. 15:16-22). These laws concerning the male were
conveniently forgotten by the church. While menstrual blood
might impede a woman's *receiving* communion, the emission
of semen was no impedient to a man's *celebrating* it!

It was apparently this immemorial abhorrence of "female"
blood that led Ambrose and Augustine to affirm that the body
of the Virgin remained closed in giving birth to Jesus.[72] This
in spite of the express mention in Luke of the ritual cleansing
(καθαρισμός) of Mary and the infant Jesus, and the latter's pre-
sentation to the Lord in fulfillment of the law respecting "every
male that *opens* the womb" (Lu. 2:22-24).[73]

And one wonders if these matters are all in the past. The
motu proprio released by Pope Paul under date of September
14, 1972, reserves ordination to the ministries of lector and
acolyte to men, according to the "venerable tradition of the
church." And it does so on the advice of the bishops, the majority of whom, it is reported, felt that women should be barred
from staying too close to the altar.[74] As it was once believed
that the relationship between Virgin and Child was too intimate to allow the defiling flow of female blood in birth, so it
is now believed, it would seem, that this defiling flow proscribes
an intimate relationship to the altar which is sanctified by the
body and blood of the same Child.

Second Addendum: Was Jesus Married?

Though our present study is concerned with the man/
woman relationship in a broader context than that of marriage,
yet the critical importance of Jesus' relationship to women
warrants our turning aside briefly to discuss the question raised

---

72. See Simone de Beauvoir's comment, *The Second Sex*, p. 156.

73. See Ex. 13:2, 12, 15. Not only menstruation but also giving birth rendered the Jewish woman ritually unclean (Lev. 2:22).

74. See *The Los Angeles Times*, Fri., Sept. 15, 1972, Part I, p. 1.

by William E. Phipps, in his study entitled *Was Jesus Married?*
This question was answered in the affirmative by some of the
founding fathers of the Mormon Church; in fact, they argued
that Jesus was married more than once.

> Brigham Young, in one of his sermons . . . declared that
> "Jesus Christ was a practical polygamist; Mary and Mar-
> tha, the sisters of Lazarus, were his plural wives, and Mary
> Magdalene was another. Also, the bridal feast at Cana of
> Galilee, where Jesus turned the water into wine, was on
> the occasion of one of his own weddings."[75]

This bit of early American theology has not been generally
adopted, and with reason, since the Gospels make it indubitably
clear that Jesus was firmly committed to monogamy. No responsible scholar would suggest that he was a polygamist. But
the question, "Was Jesus ever married?" is not so easily dis-
patched. To this question, in striking contrast to tradition, Phipps
gives an all-but-affirmative answer. He deems it nearly certain
that Jesus was married sometime before his public ministry
began. Whether or not his wife was still living when he em-
barked on his itinerant ministry and, if so, whether she ever
traveled with him, is less certain. In view of the silence of the
sources, Phipps concludes that it is unlikely that Jesus was married at this time. For the same reason — silence of the sources —
he likewise concludes that Jesus never fathered children.

Phipps' case, in brief, is as follows: Jesus, as orthodox
Christianity teaches, was fully human. Furthermore, he was
thoroughly Jewish. Therefore, in the light of Jewish marital
custom, he surely must have been married. In Phipps' view,
the probability that this conclusion is correct is so high that
it cannot be neutralized by the silence of the evangelists, since
they have nothing to say about those early years of his life
when his espousal and marriage would have occurred.

In contrast to the Jewish cultural milieu which molded
Jesus' life style as a Palestinian Jew stands Greco-Roman dualism. This pagan dualism, according to Phipps, is the source of
sexual asceticism in early Christianity. Beginning with the second century, this alien, unbiblical approach to sex made its way
into Gentile Christian thought via such sources as the *Didache*

75. Orson Hyde, *Journal of Discourses of Brigham Young,* 4 (1857), p. 259,
as quoted by Phipps, *Was Jesus Married?* (New York: Harper, 1970), p. 10.

and the *Shepherd of Hermas* and the writings of such influential spokesmen as Justin, Tatian, Tertullian, Irenaeus, and others. This ascetic tendency culminated in medieval monasticism and the celibate ideal for the priesthood. From Augustine onward this ideal was fortified by a theology of original sin, the taint of which was transmitted through procreation. Given such a theology, the sex act itself tended to become identified with the lust of the flesh that wars against the human spirit in its aspirations after God.

Though the Protestant Reformers repudiated permanent vows of celibacy as unbiblical and affirmed the family as God's ordinance, they still regarded marriage as in some way a necessary antidote to fallen man's passion, making it quite unthinkable that the sinless Jesus should have entered into such a relationship. In fact, it is regarded as improper to discuss Jesus' sexual life, Phipps complains, a taboo which the most liberated, informed, and objective scholarship has not violated. Phipps concludes that it is high time the church candidly appraised the evidence about Jesus' marital status since ". . . the traditions . . . recorded in the authoritative New Testament sources point toward a married Jesus"; since life-long celibacy is "completely foreign to the biblical outlook"; and since "Hellenistic sexual asceticism, . . . responsible for the dogma that Jesus was perpetually virginal," is a "virus," a "malignancy" that has "eaten like a cancer into the body of Christ, causing sick attitudes and practices."[76]

As a piece of critical, historical research, one must commend the author's investigation for its thoroughness. But thoroughness has not always delivered the argument from an unfortunate *tendenz*, a determination to make all the evidence point in one direction. An example of this is the author's understanding of the saying of Jesus: "There are eunuchs who have made themselves eunuchs for the sake of the kingdom of heaven" (Mt. 19:12). After several pages of explanation the author comes to the conclusion: "The thrust of this saying is that permanent marriage is sanctioned, not permanent virginity." In other words, to make oneself a eunuch for the kingdom of heaven's sake it is requisite that one be married! This novel exposition is reinforced with the added comment:

76. Phipps, *Was Jesus Married?*, p. 186.

The contextual meaning of both Matthew 19:12 and of Luke 14:26 suggests that John Erskine's intuition of Jesus' personal life may have been accurate. Perhaps Jesus descended into the hell of having to endure — as did Socrates — a bitchy hussy. Or, like Hosea, he could have felt the pangs of separation from a prodigal spouse. Yet he was faithful to her, hoping that she would respond to his love. The evangelists, writing a half century later and coming from areas outside of Nazareth, may not even have been aware of these circumstances that could have been a part of Jesus' preitinerating life.[77]

Other instances of bending the evidence to favor the hypothesis are contained in the author's exposition of Pauline thought. Consider, for example, I Corinthians 7:8: "But I say to the unmarried and the widows, it is good for them if they remain even as I." According to Phipps, this is a faulty translation which obscures the fact that the Greek actually suggests that Paul, the chief interpreter of Jesus, was himself a married man. Phipps translates the Greek (ἄγαμοι) as "de-married persons" after the analogy of I Corinthians 7:11 where the same Greek word ἄγαμος refers to Christian women separated from their husbands: "But I say to the de-married persons and the widows, it is good for them if they remain even as I." Obviously such exposition is a case of special pleading, since those addressed in verse 8 are advised in verse 9 to marry if they cannot contain themselves. This counsel of marriage in the case of incontinence presupposes that one is unmarried, not de-married. True, some of those whom the apostle addresses in verse 10 as married (γεγαμηκόσιν) could be described as "de-married" since they were separated from their spouses. But these are not counseled to get married but to be reconciled to their spouses (v. 11).

Tied in with the problem of tendenz in the argument is the problem of irrelevant data. So eager is the author to marshal evidence in favor of his thesis that he overwhelms the reader with a somewhat pedantic heap of detail, much of which is well taken but beside the point. Such, in our opinion, is the mass of material bearing on the attitudes of the church toward sex in various eras of history and the premium placed on celi-

77. Phipps, *Was Jesus Married?* p. 91.

bacy as the highest virtue qualifying one for citizenship in the kingdom of heaven. To be sure, the praise of celibacy has traditionally been associated with a prudish attitude toward sex, an attitude which conceives of Jesus as though he were above sexual impulses or feelings. Phipps' effort to correct such a view is all well and good. But is it germane? He might answer, "Yes, it is definitely germane. Only when the church has affirmed Jesus' sexuality and recognized his maleness will the church seriously entertain the evidence for his marriage." At this point his argument becomes unconvincing to this writer.

To reason that orthodox doctrine teaches that our Savior was true man (*vere homo*), therefore he must have been all that is meant by the word "male" in contrast to "female," is to reason well. But this needed affirmation of Jesus' sexuality does not entail his marriage. Phipps, of course, does not argue in so many words that sexuality entails marriage; but he does argue that one of the primary reasons for the tradition that Jesus was unmarried is the church's negative attitude towards sexuality. Therefore, if the church were to correct its view of sexuality, it would have no problem with the thought that Jesus was married.

The trouble with this reasoning is that it is inaccurate. Even if the church had wholly accepted the sexual implications of the doctrine that Jesus was *vere homo*, it would not have concluded that he was married, and for profound reasons. That Phipps does not deal with these theological matters reflects his condescending and shallow reading of Christian theology, specifically Christology. And this is why his argument has the quality of irrelevance.[78] As we see it, Phipps' basic christological assumption is that our Lord was a human being fully and completely; specifically, that he was a first-century Palestinian Jew. Therefore, the proper understanding of Jesus is gained by a critical analysis of the historical process of which he was the product. Phipps begins, elaborates, and concludes his argument for a married Jesus by simply assuming that one needs

78. See Phipps, *Was Jesus Married?*, ch. 3, "The Sexuality of Jesus." In this same chapter, for example, the author expends no little effort to refute the virgin birth, a doctrine contributing, in his judgment, to the notion that Jesus never married. Now it may be that in some forms of popular piety our Lord's virgin birth is thought to imply his virgin life. But in the serious theology of the church these two ideas are not so related.

only to affirm that Jesus was true man (*vere homo*) without any reference to the fact that orthodox doctrine also affirms that he was true God (*vere Deus*). For Phipps, not the vertical but the horizontal dimension is the key to all that the church can know and ought to believe about Jesus. Phipps does not say this in so many words but his methodology unmistakably presupposes it.

If one grant his christological assumptions, his argument is a plausible one, for all of its irrelevant detail and tendentious handling of the data. If Jesus was only and essentially a first-century Palestinian Jew, then in all likelihood he was married. But if he was the Word made flesh who dwelt among us (Jo. 1:14), then in his person the kingdom of heaven is present, the kingdom in which "they neither marry nor are given in marriage" (Lu. 20:34-36). In its Old Testament preparatory form, to be sure, the kingdom did imply for the Jewish male the responsibility to propagate the seed of Abraham through marriage and paternity. But in Jesus the promise of the seed is fulfilled (Gal. 3:16); the heir of David's throne, whose kingdom knows no end, has come (Lu. 1:32-34).

Not the earthly Jewish form of the kingdom, then, but its final eschatological form provides the perspective from which to understand the New Testament portrayal of Jesus. In this form of the kingdom, the blessing is not upon the womb that bears nor the breasts that give suck, but upon those who hear and keep the word of God. Such are Jesus' true sisters, brothers and mothers (Lu. 3:35). To believe that he was unmarried is not to deny *his* humanity, but to affirm that the sexual congress of husband and wife is not an essential part of *our* humanity. In the ultimate fulfillment of Man's life in the world to come, when we shall be truly like God and enjoy him forever, men will be men and women, women — truly and completely — but they will not be husbands and wives, they will not procreate.[79]

79. Phipps construes appeal to the saying of Jesus that in the resurrection they neither marry nor are given in marriage as an instance of the "proof-text" method, tantamount to affirming that sexless angelic life should be copied in this present earthly life. "Actually," he declares, "Jesus' reply to the Sadducees can more properly be used to encourage marriage than to authorize celibacy" (*Was Jesus Married?*, pp. 92f.). Another bit of exegesis more novel than convincing.

Ultimately, then, it is not pagan Greek asceticism, but the structure of biblical revelation itself, that explains why the Jesus Christ portrayed in the Gospels and confessed by the church was a man in the literal sexual sense of the word, yet a man who did not continue the holy genealogies of Israel as devout first-century Jewish men aspired to do. Rather he is the man whose birth culminates and completes these genealogies (Mt. 1:1-17; Lu. 3:23-38) because he is the heavenly bridegroom who, though taken from his bride for a time (Mk. 2:18f.), will return to celebrate his nuptial feast at the final consummation of all things (Rev. 19:5f.).

Paralleling the affirmation of Jesus that in the fulfilled kingdom men and women will neither marry nor be given in marriage is the comment of Paul (to which we have referred above) to the same effect (I Cor. 7:25-35). Since the new age has already broken into this age, the apostle, anticipating its imminent fulfillment in the return of Christ, advised that unmarried couples should remain so, since the time would soon come when those having wives would be as those having none.[80] And, of course, when that time comes, then we shall be like Jesus our Lord, for we shall see him as he is.

F. The Pauline Argument Revisited

1. Introduction

We have suggested that Barth's theology of Man as male and female contains an antinomy: The woman is man's partner in life, equal to him in every way; yet she is subordinate to him in an irrevocable way. She stands on the same plane with the man, yet under him. In the older theological tradition no such antinomy was felt, since the inferiority which female subordination implies was not denied but rather affirmed. The woman stands under the man because she is under him. Barth,

---

80. Phipps' comment on this aspect of Paul's teaching is that his "early eschatological fervor later cooled." Like Plato, Goethe, and "other great intellectuals," as his theology "matured" the apostle "changed his mind" — in the direction of Phipps' theology, of course. "Paul's most mature thought on this subject is contained in Ephesians, where there is no hint of preference for the unmarried state" (Was Jesus Married?, pp. 109, 117).

however, will not go this far. In fact his basic thought is in the other direction; woman is in no way inferior to man. Hence the antinomy in his affirmation that she is nonetheless subordinate to him because she is woman.

We have further suggested that the character of redemptive history itself throws light on this antinomy. Because the society of ancient Israel was patriarchal, the man used the opportunity which such a societal pattern afforded him to dominate the woman, reducing her to the inferior status of a second-class citizen in the covenant community. Jesus, by contrast, though he was a man, never dominated women nor treated them as inferior. In his presence there were no "emancipated ladies" who were "put in their place." Rather they were *truly* emancipated; *their place was the human place.* Hence in the new Israel, which he is creating by his Spirit, there is no room for the thought that the male is superior to the female and therefore ought to have the rule over her.

The apostle Paul was the heir of this contrast between the old and the new. To understand his thought about the relation of the woman to the man, one must appreciate that he was both a Jew and a Christian. He was a rabbi of impeccable erudition who had become an ardent disciple of Jesus Christ. And his thinking about women — their place in life generally and in the church specifically — reflects both his Jewish and his Christian experience. The traditional teaching of Judaism and the revolutionary new approach implied in the life and teaching of Jesus contributed, each in its own way, to the apostle's thinking about the relationship of the sexes. So far as he thought in terms of his Jewish background, he thought of the woman as subordinate to the man for whose sake she was created (I Cor. 11:9). But so far as he thought in terms of the new insight he had gained through the revelation of God in Christ, he thought of the woman as equal to the man in all things, the two having been made one in Christ, in whom there is neither male nor female (Gal. 3:28).

2. *Intrinsic Problems*

Because these two perspectives — the Jewish and the Christian — are incompatible, there is no satisfying way to harmonize the Pauline argument for female subordination with the larger Christian vision of which the great apostle to the Gentiles was himself the primary architect. It appears from the evidence that Paul himself sensed that his view of the man/woman relationship, inherited from Judaism, was not altogether congruous with the gospel he preached.

For one thing, in the very passage where he most emphatically affirms female subordination he makes an interesting parenthetical remark. Though he will not say that the woman is the image and glory of God, but only that she is the glory of the man (I Cor. 11:7), he nonetheless affirms that as the woman is not without the man, so the man is not without the woman, in the Lord. For even as the woman is of (ἐκ) the man, so the man is through (διά) the woman. And all things are of God (I Cor. 11:11-12).[81]

Here the apostle appears to hint that "in the Lord," that is, in the fellowship of the gospel, the man and the woman are more nearly equal than his insistence upon a hierarchical relationship of the sexes would imply. He sees a pointer in the direction of equality in the fact that though the first woman was created from the man, all men, subsequently, are born of women. When a Christian man, then, is thinking about the fact that the first woman came from a man, he ought not forget that God has so arranged things that he, a man, was born of a woman. If the first woman owed her existence to the first man from whom she was taken, all other men owe their existence to those women who conceived them and brought them into the world. Thus the score is somewhat evened up. Here we have what may be the first expression of an uneasy conscience on the part of a Christian theologian who argues for the subordination of the female to the male by virtue of her derivation from the male.

If the apostle's observation that the sexes are mutually de-

81. The fact that the apostle uses the same preposition διά in vv. 9 and 12 of I Cor. 11 does not, of course, mean that he is saying the man is "for the sake of" the woman as the woman is "for the sake of the man." Such an exposition would be grammatically impossible since the preposition occurs in the first instance with the accusative, in the second with the genitive, case. It only obscures the issue, therefore, to skirt v. 9 and stress v. 12, as commentators are prone to do when they cannot agree with the apostle yet do not want to disagree with him either.

pendent suggests some difficulty in his reasoning concerning the headship of the male, so, more obviously, do his statements about female participation in the service of public worship. In I Corinthians 11 he plainly allows that if she covers her head the woman like the man may lead the congregation in prayer and exhort the members thereof with a word of prophecy (v. 5). However, in I Corinthians 14:34-35, he says that the woman is to keep silence in the church as an expression of her sub-jection, a silence required by the law itself. The law, however, nowhere says this. Some have suggested that Paul may have in mind Genesis 3:16: "Your desire shall be to your husband, and he shall have the rule over you." But were one to reason from this text (which is a part of the curse on fallen woman) that she ought to be silently submissive to the man, then one should also reason that the man, who stands under the same condemnation, should not struggle (with the help of tech-nology) against the thorns and thistles that infest the ground!

Surely the apostle knew the Scripture too well to turn a curse into a commandment, a judgment into a mandate. Such a text as Genesis 3:16 describes, as Phyllis Trible has observed, it does not prescribe; it protests, it does not condone.[82] Hence one can only suppose that the apostle's remarks in I Corinthians 14:34-35 reflect the rabbinic tradition which imposed silence on the woman in the synagogue as a sign of her subjection. The law enjoined silence upon the woman in public worship only in the sense that rabbinic authority so construed it by way of a general implication.

Some scholars have plausibly suggested, in view of these difficulties, that this passage is the interpolation of a later hand. In the best critical text of the Greek Testament, the editors, using a scale of A-D in rating doubtful texts, note that I Corin-thians 14:34-35 is a B text, that is, a text having "some degree of doubt." However, the doubt is not sufficient to prevent most

82. See her "Depatriarchalizing in Biblical Interpretation," Journal of the American Academy of Religion, 41 (March, 1973), p. 41. In contrast to Phyllis Trible's perceptive remark, consider the following: "The first com-mandment which God gave unto the woman was, 'Thy desire shall be to thy husband and he shall rule over thee'" (Fascinating Womanhood, Helen B. Andelin, Santa Barbara, 18th printing, 1971, p. 89). To find a curse on woman called a commandment is surprising; to find such a mis-take in a book written for women, more surprising; to learn that the author is herself a woman, more surprising still.

interpreters from attempting to alleviate the seeming contradiction by one means or another. Older expositors sometimes
denied that I Corinthians 11:5 allowed women to pray or
prophesy in church with covered heads. Rather (as Calvin
argued) we must recognize that the apostle could deal with
only one problem at a time. First he gives the reason why
women should wear a veil (I Cor. 11) and then why they should
keep silent in church (I Cor. 14). Today such a position is not
taken; rather it is frequently suggested that Paul did not mean
that all women should always keep silent, but only those who
were disturbing the worship by their unedifying and too-fre-
quent questions.[83] Not only does such a harmonizing effort lack
historical proof, but it implies that men, in contrast to women,
never offended in this respect, at least not so as to warrant an
apostolic admonition. As an expository solution such a view
leaves something to be desired.

While feminine silence was literally observed in the Jewish
synagogue, it seems that it was not observed in the churches
of the apostolic age. Even Paul, who speaks in I Corinthians
14:34-35 (if the text is authentic) in a way that reflects his
Jewish scruples, allowed that women could offer prayer or
prophesy in a public service of worship — so long as they had
their heads covered (I Cor. 11:5). Different churches in different ages have engaged in similar compromises. Women have
been allowed to sing in virtually all churches, though they
have not been allowed to select hymns or lead in the singing
in *some* churches (as in certain Brethren assemblies).[84] In *some*
churches they not only sing, but pray in the midweek prayer
meeting (otherwise many prayer meetings would be *sans*
prayers); yet they may not lead in the pastoral prayer on Sunday morning. In any case, whether singing in the choir of a

83. So Oepke, "γυνή," *TDNT,* I, p. 788, though admitting the critical problem with the text. However one may explain I Cor. 14:34-35, I Tim. 2:9f.
remains. In fact, the easier one makes it to harmonize I Cor. 14 with I Cor.
11, the more difficult he makes it to harmonize I Cor. 14 with I Tim. 2.

84. Some now extinct Baptist churches prohibited singing altogether, by
either sex. But even those Baptists who approved singing sometimes pro-
scribed *female* singing, along with the use of instruments, as unscriptural.
See Percy A. Scholes, *The Oxford Companion to Music* (London: Oxford
Univ. Press, 1970), p. 83.

modern church or praying in the assembly of an apostolic church, women have never been completely silent.

To soften the problems created by the literal meaning of I Corinthians 14:34-35, contemporary translations indulge a little scholarly interpretation with interesting results. *The New English Bible* reads:

> And in all congregations of God's people, women should not *address the meeting*. They have no license to speak, but should keep their place as the law directs. If there is something they want to know, they can ask their own husbands at home. It is a shocking thing that a woman should *address the congregation*.

This translation does not require that women keep absolutely still in church. They may speak, but not as leaders who address the congregation after the analogy of the leader in the synagogue who expounds the Scripture. Were one to paraphrase the text in terms of the form of Protestant worship common in our day, it would read something like this: "Women should not preach the Sunday sermon, for it is a shocking thing that a woman should preach the sermon to the gathered congregation." But even this salvo will not make the apostle quite consistent with himself, for, as we have noted, he allows women to "prophesy" in church, which had a similar place in the worship of his day to "preaching the sermon" in ours.[85]

It is not just in I Corinthians 14:34-35 that the injunction to female silence is given. In I Timothy 2:11-15 it is also found, and in this passage the reasons for it are spelled out in a way that defies hermeneutical ingenuity. Quiet subjection to the man is required of the woman because, as the second to be created, it was she, not the man, who was deceived by the tempter.

Whether or not this passage be construed as Pauline, it must be said to the apostle's credit that he never speaks elsewhere of the woman in such a way. Though he mentions the example of Eve's being deceived by the serpent (II Cor. 11:3), his fear is not that the men of Corinth will suffer from

85. The suggestion is sometimes made that in I Cor. 14:34 the apostle proscribes only the woman's speaking in tongues, not prayer and prophecy. This is because of the supposed predilection of the female to emotional excesses. Aside from the unwarranted stereotype, the context allows of no such interpretation. Prophecy, not tongues, is the subject of the immediately preceding verses (31-33).

their commerce with Eve's daughters, but rather that Satan, being a master of deceit, may lead the whole congregation astray in like manner. Steeped in rabbinic learning though he was, the apostle did not blame the woman for the fall of the man, as did the ancient Fathers of the church. It was not *she* who was in transgression (I Tim. 2:14) but Man, according to his argument in Romans. It was through one human being (δι' ἑνὸς ἀνθρώπου) that sin entered into the world, and death by sin (Rom. 5:12).[86]

Traditionally, however, the theologians of the church have not shown this apostolic restraint. For over a thousand years they made this argument from the deception of the woman the basis of a demeaning theology of womanhood. When alone in the garden, without the man, the woman succumbed to the tempter's wiles and thus led the whole human race to perdition. In the words of Jesus, son of Sirach: "Woman is the origin of sin, and it is through her that we all die."[87] This lamentable display on the woman's part of inferior moral integrity and intellectual acumen is proof positive that the woman should be subordinate to the man.

There is, needless to say, no hint of all this in the biblical narrative of the fall. One might just as well reason that the tempter approached the woman because he knew her to be the key to the situation as the more astute. Of course few have even suggested this latter interpretation, and the reason is not far to seek. But it has as much (and as little) intrinsic worth as the view which censures the woman as the ruin of the man.[88]

Returning to the Pauline argument for female subordination, besides the difficulties already mentioned, there is the problematic appeal which the apostle makes to the woman's veil and long hair as reflecting a law of nature (I Cor. 11:14-15).

86. When the apostle traces the sin of mankind back to the "disobedience of the one" in Rom. 5:18-19, this, of course, is not to blame the man instead of the woman. He speaks in the singular because of the contrast and comparison with Christ, the one man who accomplished our salvation.

87. Ecclesiasticus 25:24-25, *New English Bible*.

88. Certain Roman Catholic theologians, who pursue a mystical understanding of the feminine principle as passivity and openness to God (the function of the Virgin), have, indeed, argued that the tempter attacked, not the weaker vessel, but the "most powerful religious principle of creation," after which the man's ruin was easily achieved. So Willi Moll, *Die Dreifach Antwort der Liebe* (Graz: Verlag Styria, 1964). See below, Epilogue: The Ontology of Sex, pp. 171ff.

For him these customs of wearing the hair long and of veiling the head express, as it were in symbol, the absolute will of God. Hence he is anything but indifferent to them, for they are divinely appointed signs of male authority which the woman is obligated to respect as the one created for the sake of the man (vv. 9-10). Therefore the apostle's remark (v. 16) that the churches of God have no such "custom" (συνήθεια) of women unveiling themselves during public worship cannot mean that he regarded the whole matter as *mere* custom. Though one may argue that such indeed is the case, one cannot say that this is what the text means.

Quite the contrary, this particular custom, in the thinking of Paul, was part of the apostolic tradition which he had given them and by which they were bound. This, in fact, is the note on which he opens the whole discussion, praising them for holding fast the traditions (παραδόσεις) "even as I delivered them to you" (v. 2). Thus the apostle elevates the relativities of culture to the absolutes of Christian piety. Even here, however, the church, dominated by males, has been slow to acknowledge the inadequacy of the argument. Bobbed hair, bossy wives, and women preachers have been lumped together in a common condemnation in many a sermon taken from I Cor. 11, while those with a penchant for erudition have appealed to an alleged cultural consensus that women should wear long hair.[89]

89. Sermons against bobbed hair having proved ineffectual, the opposite tack is sometimes taken: that Paul's argument for the covering of the female head was intended to be an argument for the times only, since prostitutes did not wear a veil or long hair in the apostle's day. This was why it was important that the women of the Corinthian church *should* do so as Christians, though Christian women today are not so obligated. There is neither a hint in the text of I Corinthians nor evidence in the context of first-century Corinthian life for this curious idea. In the only passage where Scripture dilates on the dress of a prostitute, so far from being uncovered, her identity could not be discerned. Judah thought Tamar, his daughter-in-law, to be a harlot "because she had *covered* her face" (Gen. 38:15). Cf. Oepke, "κατακαλύπτω," *TDNT*, III, pp. 561-563.

In recent times the church has had more to say about the long hair of men than the short hair of women. For some easy reading, with ample illustrations, see *Campus Life*, Feb. 1972, "The Great Hair Hassle," pp. 18f. D. L. Moody, it seems, could not now enroll in Moody Bible Institute! According to a *Los Angeles Times* report (Tues., Aug. 29, 1972), Greek Orthodox monks on Mt. Athos, having traditionally banned even female animals from their peninsula, have now forbidden access to long-haired men as well, since they look like women!

Finally, all the Pauline texts supporting female subordination, both those that are directly from the apostle's pen and those that are indirectly so, appeal to the second creation narrative, Genesis 2:18-23, never to the first. This fact should not be overlooked, for it relates to a significant theological matter. Whereas the Bible begins its doctrine of Man with the fundamental affirmation that "God created Man in his own image, in the image of God created he him, male and female created he them" (Gen. 1:27) and regards the account of the woman's creation from the rib of the man as supplementing this fundamental affirmation, Paul hardly ever refers to Genesis 1:27. Both in I Corinthians and in I Timothy appeal is made only to the second creation narrative as the sole text for understanding the meaning of human existence as male and female. Thus this second, supplementary narrative is interpreted in isolation from the first. The reason for saying that "the man is the image and glory of God, but the woman the glory of the man" (I Cor. 11:7) is that, according to Genesis 2, "The man is not out of the woman, but the woman out of the man" (11:8). And it is for this same reason that the woman should veil her head (11:10) and learn in silence (I Tim. 2:12-13).[90]

Furthermore, in reasoning this way, Paul is not only basing his argument exclusively on the second creation narrative, but is assuming the traditional rabbinic understanding of that narrative whereby the order of their creation is made to yield the primacy of the man over the woman. Is this rabbinic understanding of Genesis 2:18f. correct? We do not think that it is, for it is palpably inconsistent with the first creation narrative, with the life style of Jesus, and with the apostle's own clear affirmation that in Christ there is no male and female (Gal. 3:28). In reaching this conclusion, we come to the crux of the matter where careful elaboration is needed. We shall begin this elaboration with an analysis of the second creation narrative. How should one understand Genesis 2:18-23, which speaks of the woman as created from the man to be a help meet for him? What is the theological significance of this statement?

90. It is, of course, true that Gen. 1:27 is obliquely referred to in the apostle's speaking of the man as the image and glory of God.

G. An Analysis of the Second Creation Narrative

"Eve was not taken from the feet of Adam to be his slave, nor from his head to be his lord, but from his side to be his partner."[91] This beautiful sentiment reflects the imagery of the second creation account (Gen. 2:18-23), a narrative which Karl Barth has called the Magna Carta of our humanity.[92]

According to this narrative, the Lord God said:

(18) It is not good that man should be alone; I will make him a help answering to him. (19) And the Lord God formed all the beasts of the field out of the ground, and the birds of the heaven, and brought them to the man to see what he would call them. . . . (20) And the man gave names to all. . . . But for man there was not found a help answering to him. (21) And the Lord God caused a deep sleep to fall upon the man and he slept, and he took one of his ribs and closed up its place with flesh. (22) And the rib which the Lord God had taken from the man he made into a woman and brought her to the man. (23) And the man said: This at last is bone of my bone and flesh of my flesh, she shall be called woman because she was taken out of man.

To this story of the woman's creation the Genesis narrative immediately subjoins a significant observation which has to do with the ordinance of marriage. It is, the narrative says, because of the relationship between man and woman established by creation that a man is to leave his father and mother and cleave to his wife that they may become one flesh (Gen. 2:24). It is very important, as we have already observed, to note this distinction between the account of the woman's creation as given in vv. 18-23 and the relationship of marriage described in v. 24. The former involves an act of God; the latter an act of Man. The former is the primary fact, the latter the secondary fact, in a Christian view of Man as male and female.

While this distinction between the creation of male and female, on the one hand, and the institution of marriage, on the other, is reflected in the structure of the text itself, obviously it was not as important to the Old Testament writers as it has

91. Peter Lombard, *Sentent.*, 1. II. Dist. XVIII, quoted by P. Schaff, *Church History*, II, p. 363.
92. Barth, *K.D.*, III/2, § 45, p. 351 [291].

become in the Christian view of life. In the thought of ancient Israel and later Judaism, the creation of the woman as man's partner in life simply merged with the marriage relationship. The story of God's giving the woman to the man became, for all practical purposes, the first wedding. In Jewish thought, as a matter of fact, the man who remained unmarried was really an incomplete and unfinished man; he was like the Adam of the creation story who found no helper suitable for him. And the woman who did not have a husband was simply disgraced. According to Isaiah, in a day when the ranks of the men shall be decimated by war, "seven women shall take hold of one man, saying: 'We will eat our own bread and wear our own clothes, only let us be called by your name; take away our reproach'" (Is. 4:1).

In other words, in the Old Testament as a whole, the *presupposition* of marriage merges with the *reality* of marriage. In the Jewish Scriptures the man and the woman, in their mutual relationship, are viewed almost exclusively as husband and wife and as father and mother. Were one to seek a theological explanation for this absorbing preoccupation of the Old Testament with marriage and the family, perhaps the best suggestion that can be made is that the covenant promise given to Abraham of a numerous seed, a seed in whom all the nations should be blessed, made it necessary to place the primary emphasis on the institution by which the holy generations of Israel were preserved till the Messiah should come, who is the Seed of Abraham *par excellence* (Gal. 3:16f.). But now that he has come the situation has changed; the genealogies with which Matthew and Luke introduce Jesus' life are the last to be recorded in the Bible. He has come in whose person the kingdom of heaven is present, and in this kingdom "they neither marry nor are given in marriage."[93]

Turning to the direct exposition of the text of Genesis 2:18-23, a word is in order about the character of the narrative. Traditionally it has been taken as a literal piece of historical

93. In the thought of the church, the meaning of womanhood has remained largely synonymous with motherhood. The woman is "fulfilled" in becoming a mother in a way that is not true of the man in becoming a father. For a balanced and perceptive analysis of the biblical data on motherhood, from a Christian perspective, see Charlotte von Kirchbaum, *Die Wirkliche Frau* (Zurich: Evangelischer Verlag, 1949), pp. 51f.

reporting. Understood in this manner, the passage has had an interesting secondary history. For centuries it was the basis of the doubtful anatomical theory that the male of the human species was minus a rib on one side. In fact, when Andreas Vesalius, a founder of the science of anatomy, dissected a cadaver and disputed the point, the church condemned him to exile (1564) not only for his temerity but especially for his heresy. Somewhat later (1847) this same text, which was the undoing of Vesalius, proved the salvation of the eminent Scottish physician and surgeon James Simpson. Beleaguered with controversy over his use of anesthesia to deaden the pain of childbirth — a circumvention of the divine will, as it was supposed — Simpson pacified his distractors by appealing to the "deep sleep" which the Lord God had caused to fall upon the man as the first surgical operation.[94]

With the establishment of biology and anthropology as empirical sciences, such a literal interpretation of the Genesis account of woman's creation no longer commends itself, a result which in no way alters the significance of the narrative as a divine revelation. In fact, the frequently alleged contradiction between this narrative with its view of the *successive* creation of the male and the female and the first narrative which speaks of them as created *simultaneously* (Gen. 1:27) is of no account when the text is understood not as a literal piece of scientific reporting but as a narrative which illumines the ultimate meaning of Man's existence in the dual form of male and female.

The narrative in Genesis 2:18-23 is commonly classified by scholars as a religious "myth" or "saga" in the sense that it clothes the truth about the origin of man and woman in poetic or parabolic form.[95] However, it is markedly different in content from its pagan counterparts. In the myth of the androgyne,

94. "Probably the most absurd argument by which a great cause was ever won," comments Andrew Dickson White, *The History of the Warfare of Science with Theology in Christendom* (New York: Appleton, 1955), II, p. 63.

95. There is hardly a satisfactory term to describe technically the Genesis narrative. The common scholarly designation, "etiological myth," conveys the misleading notion of a fictitious story written after the fact to explain the status quo, like Plato's "myth" of the androgyne. Even the word "saga," used by Barth, implies legendary embellishment of a historical kernel. Hence we have preferred the term "narrative" in the sense of a recital of events in the form of a story.

for example, as reported in Plato's *Symposium*, Zeus split original men in two "like a sorb-apple which is halved for pickling,"
each half a man or a woman, because of the insolence of original
men in daring to scale heaven that they might lay hands on
the gods. Significantly, in the biblical narrative the division of
the original Man (who is called *adham*, אדם) into a man and
a woman (called an *ish*, איש, and an *ishshah*, אשה) is not a
judgment upon Man for his sin but a creative act of God, per-
formed because Man's very nature is such that it is not good
that he should be alone.[96] It is in the Garden of Eden, the
biblical allegory of the bliss of God's favor which man enjoyed
before he fell, that the mysterious division takes place resulting
in man and woman. Sexuality, then, is not the result of the
fall; it is not a judgment, a rending asunder of that essential
being which can be what it is intended to be only in unity.[97]
Rather there is an ontological distinction in the being of Man
wrought by a creative act of God, this distinction being person-
alized sexuality as man and woman.

That the difference between man and woman is due to an
act of God is seen, in the story, in the deep sleep which comes
upon Adam while God works mysteriously to make Man into
man and woman. We cannot say exactly why a "rib" (הצלה)
is mentioned. It has been suggested that the bodily member
concerned should be a bone, as a solid and substantial part,
and what could be more appropriate than the bone which en-
closes and shelters the breast and heart where the deepest and
noblest affections reside?

More important than the precise significance of the "rib"
(which is likely not intended to have any precise significance)

96. Broadly speaking, *adham* is the generic word in Hebrew for Man
(mankind) while *ish* denotes the human male. In Hebrew, however, as in
English, "man" and "mankind" are assimilated. Hebrew usage is further
complicated by the fact that the same word *adham* is also used as a proper
name, "Adam," to designate an individual male, as in the phrase, "Adam
knew Eve his wife" (Gen. 4:25). This complexity is illustrated in Gen.
5:1-2, which reads: "This is the book of the generations of Adam [*man*,
mankind]. When God created Adam [*man*, mankind] he made him in the
likeness of God. Male and female he created them and he blessed them
and named them Adam [*man*, mankind] when they were created." We
have italicized the different translations, as they appear in current English
versions, of the same Hebrew word.

97. See above, pp. 24ff., for our criticism of the androgynous ideal.

is the fact that at this point in the narrative the sexual factor, in the narrower sense of the word, recedes into the background. Woman is not a man without a penis, as Freud crudely defined her; it is not the anatomical difference between the man and the woman but their essential relatedness that is emphasized. Woman is taken from the man in the sense that, being distinct from him, she is yet like him, bone of his bone and flesh of his flesh.

In this description, to be sure, the language ("bone" and "flesh") is drawn from the physical realm; there is a bodily likeness between the man and the woman. But this does not mean that the woman is like the man only or principally at the biological level in contrast to the spiritual realm. She is described by God, her Maker, as a "helper fit for him" (עזר כנגדו), the preposition (כ + נגד) meaning "corresponding to," "equal and adequate to." She is the "help of his like," to translate literally; or, to paraphrase in the words of Delitzsch, she is a "helping being, in which, as soon as he sees her, the man recognizes himself."

Significantly, too, there is no suggestion that she is a helper in a particular way, as the bearer of children (Augustine) or the keeper of the home, to speak of the two most common feminine stereotypes. Many women have borne children and kept the home in other generations, and many will continue to do so in the future. And this has been and always will be according to God's will. But this is not the will of God for *every* woman by definition. To say that childbearing is "what she was made for" in an exclusive way that bars the woman from the larger partnership of human life is an arrogant male conclusion which the text does not warrant.[98]

The woman is not described as the man's servant, his valet, his little errand girl whom he needs for this or that, but as the help equal and adequate to him and without whom he cannot be a man. The word for "help" in Genesis 2:18, 20 (עזר) is never used elsewhere to designate a subordinate. In fact, it is sometimes used of God himself, who is Man's help

---

98. "Taking a wife is a remedy for fornication. Women bear children and are wont to educate them and to administer domestic affairs. Moreover they are inclined to be merciful, for they are appointed by God to bear children, to please man, and to be compassionate." Martin Luther, from the *Nachschriften of* Veit Deitnch, 1531.

in time of need (see Ps. 146:5). Furthermore, as God takes counsel with himself before making Man (Gen. 1:26) and thus commends to us the dignity of our nature as human, so he takes counsel before making woman in particular (Gen. 2:8) and thus commends to us the dignity of her nature as female. It should also be noted that God is directly involved in making the woman, even as he is in making the man. Whereas plants and animals are simply called into being by a divine word, it is not so with the man and the woman. God made man by taking the dust up into his hands and stooping to breathe directly into his nostrils the breath of life (Gen. 2:7). So also, in making the woman, he took the rib and fashioned it into a woman and brought her to the man (Gen. 2:22), and so Man became man and woman.[99]

By describing the woman's creation in this manner, the account underscores the point that she is not the creation of the man. In no sense does she owe her being to him, any more than he owes his being to her. When she is created, he is in an unknowing sleep. In other words, he contributes no more to her creation than to his own creation; the mystery of her being is the same mystery as his own being. Her being is just as unmistakably her own as his being is his own; he cannot put her in his debt. Not that her being is alien to his, competing with his, for she is bone of his bone and flesh of his flesh; but her being is hers, even as his being is his, and both are given their specific being as man or woman, that as man and woman they may share life together as creatures of God uniquely endowed with the divine image. The narrative of Genesis 2 commits us to the integrity and freedom of the woman over against the man and of the man over against the woman, even as it commits us to their togetherness in an ineluctable relationship. This

99. As a result of the assimilation of the word "man" in the sense of human being to the word "man" in the sense of male of the species, the Hebrew אדם is used to designate both the man (איש) and the woman (אשה) and also to designate the man in distinction to the woman. In the days of prescientific literalism, this latter usage, which occurs in Gen. 2:7, naturally lent itself to an interpretation of the text which viewed the male as the true Man (אדם), who embodies the plenitude of humanity, apart from the woman — this in spite of the fact that the narrative expressly states later on (Gen. 2:18) that it is not good that the man (אדם) should be alone.

is the theology of the second creation narrative. As Bailey well says:

> Such a theology will thus treat chiefly of what man and woman *are*, not what they *do* — though by applying the principles and insights so established, it will attempt to elucidate the many practical problems which constantly arise in connection with the ecclesiastical, social, legal, matrimonial, and venereal [coital] relationships of the sexes.[100]

We can only conclude, therefore, that when the narrative in Genesis 2 speaks of the woman as made from the man, the intent is to distinguish her from the animals by implying her essential likeness to the one from whom she is taken. *Her superiority over the animals, not her inferiority to the man, is the fundamental thought in the immediate context.* However, when the rabbis read in Genesis 2 that the woman was made *from* the man, they came to infer from this that she was *under* the man. But such an inference is an obvious *non sequitur*; derivation does not entail subordination. Such exposition reflects the patriarchal relationship between the sexes which was an historical fact in Israel rather than the necessary meaning of the text itself. So far as Genesis 2 is concerned, sexual hierarchy must be read into the text; it is not required by the text.

That subordination does not follow from derivation can be seen from this very same narrative where it is said (Gen. 2:7) that the man was formed "out of" the ground (מן-האדמה). Who would argue that the man is subordinate to the ground because taken from it? Furthermore, even if one were to take the narrative in Genesis 2 literally so as to postulate a temporal priority in the creation of the male (Adam was *first* formed, *then* Eve, I Tim. 2:13), there is nothing in the thought of temporal priority which implies superior worth or value. So far as temporal priority is concerned, according to the first creation narrative animals were created before Man, yet this does not imply their superior worth over Man. Quite the reverse: Man, who is last, is the crown of creation and has dominion over the creatures. If one were to infer anything from the fact that the

---

100. *Sexual Relation in Christian Thought*, p. 276.

woman was created after the man, it should be, in the light
of the first creation narrative, that the woman is superior to
the man.[101] But if men do not find this conclusion palatable,
let them ask themselves why women should stomach the rabbinic conclusion that the woman is inferior because created
after the man.

Immediately subjoined to the second creation narrative is
the statement that because the woman, taken from the man,
is bone of his bone and flesh of his flesh, *therefore* shall a man
leave his father and mother and cleave to his wife and they
shall become one flesh (Gen. 2:24). Since this statement is not
per se a part of the second creation narrative, we have not dwelt
on it in the exposition of that narrative. It is a fundamental
pronouncement, not about creation, but about marriage, the
specific relationship that exists between a man and a woman
when they are joined in one flesh as husband and wife. But
it is closely associated in Genesis with the creation of the
woman and, to say the least, the form of the statement is surprising. If the implication which the rabbis drew, that the
woman is subject to the man because she is taken from the man,
is intended by the narrative, then why does not Genesis 2:24
read: "Therefore shall a *woman* leave her father and mother
and cleave unto her *husband,* and they shall become one
flesh?" This is, as a matter of fact, what always happened in the
patriarchal society of ancient Israel: the woman left her own
family to become a member of her husband's family.

Scholars have been exercised to explain this seeming dis-
crepancy between the account of the woman's creation from
the man in Genesis 2:18-23 and the fundamental statement of
the creation ordinance of marriage in Genesis 2:24. Some have
suggested that it reflects a long-forgotten matriarchal social
structure in Israel. But this is hardly a convincing hypothesis,

101. Milton puts this argument into the mouth of Adam:
    O fairest of creation, last and best
    Of all God's works, creature in whom excelled
    Whatever can to sight or thought be formed,
    Holy, divine, good, amiable, or sweet!
Paradise Lost, Bk. IX, ll. 896-899. But, of course, this is Adam about to fall,
unable to resist the charms of his consort turned temptress.

because it is wholly without evidence. Abraham, the father of
the Jewish race, was truly a patriarch, whose wife, as Peter
reminds us, addressed him as "lord" (I Pet. 3:6); and the nation descending from his loins was patriarchal through and
through. It was the woman, in such a society, who left father
and mother and clove to her husband. Yet in the original
biblical statement of the ordinance of marriage it is the man
who "leaves" and "cleaves." And these terms are very strong
ones. The verb "to leave" (עזב) means "to abandon," "to
forsake," and is used predominantly of forsaking strange gods.
And the verb "to cleave" (דבק) conveys strong personal at-
tachment, as when Ruth cleaves to Naomi (Ru. 1:14), the
people to their king (II Sam. 20:2), and (eight occurrences)
Israel to their God.

Noting that a husband and wife are bound by stronger ties
than parents to children, Heinrich Baltensweiler observes that
Genesis 2:24 is a singular formulation which contradicts the
actual procedure in Israel:

> This saying receives its real significance only when one
> recalls that the Jahvist on all other occasions represents the
> family ordinance as patriarchal. Seen in this light, the fact
> that the man is said to leave his family and "cleave unto
> his wife" can only mean that it was the intent of the
> author to rule out all lowering of the worth of the woman.
> Though it might appear, from what had gone before, that
> the man is to be looked upon as the overlord of the woman,
> yet now matters are reversed so that the man leaves all
> for the sake of his wife. He loves her so much; so much
> does the thought of her fill his mind, that he is ready to
> break the closest family ties which blood relationship can
> establish. He will cleave to his wife and they shall become
> one flesh.[102]

The argument, then, that the woman should be subject to
the man as her head because, according to Genesis 2, she was
created from the man, is not without its refutation in the
sequel to very creation narrative on which it is traditionally
based.

102. Heinrich Baltensweiler, *Die Ehe im Neuen Testament* (Zurich:
Zwingli Verlag, 1967), p. 21.

H. The Rejection of the Hierarchical View of the Man/Woman Relationship in Favor of One of Partnership

1. Introduction

As we conclude our discussion of the man/woman relationship, there are several matters that should be mentioned in the interest of clarity.

First of all, in reviewing the place of woman in the Old Testament and in Judaism, we noted that the Old Testament everywhere assumes a patriarchal structure of society as an expression of the will of God. Is the Old Testament wrong in this assumption? Not at all. In fact, in a world where superior physical prowess was required to survive, it was natural that the man should assume the primary responsibility for the family. We should not, however, absolutize patriarchy as the best possible societal structure for all ages and places any more than we should absolutize monarchy. Appealing to the divine right of the male over the female is like appealing to the divine right of kings. Both patriarchy, the rule of the father as head of the family, and monarchy, the rule of the king as head of the state, were recognized as an expression of the divine will in the Old Testament. But it does not follow that they are the only possible expression of the divine will for every time and civilization. Although the king, the "Lord's Anointed," ruled in Israel as God's vicegerent, symbolizing the theocratic fatherhood of God, yet there are other forms of the state consonant with the divine will, perhaps even more so than that which is found in the Old Testament. And by the same token there are other forms of social order consonant with the divine will besides patriarchy.

While patriarchy may be the best form of society under given circumstances, its obvious weakness is the occasion which woman's dependency affords the man to suppress her rights as a person. Dependency, to be sure, does not necessarily imply subordination. A person who is ill may be *dependent* on a physician to regain his health, but he is not *subordinate* to the physician. Yet in a *sinful* world it is unrealistic to suppose that half the human race could be made to depend on the other half without

the one abusing, the other suffering the abuse of, such a relationship. While the grace of God ameliorated such abuse in Israel,
there was abuse still.

It is only in terms of amelioration of abuse that one can
understand the revelatory character of those Old Testament
laws and customs which involve discrimination against the
woman. For example, when the ancient rite of the water of
bitterness is introduced with the solemn words, "And the Lord
spoke unto Moses" (Nu. 5:11), this can only mean that this
rite was of God so far as it stood between the wife and her
husband, lest she be destroyed without recourse by his jealous
rage. In this sense God gave Israel those laws which concerned
the treatment of women victimized by the injustices of polygamy, made destitute by the repudiation of their husbands, and
reduced to slavery as the pawns of war. Such laws do not
express the will of God for womankind in any absolute and
final sense, but rather secure a measure of justice for the oppressed and weaker sex against their unrestrained exploitation by the male. If revelation is historical — as the Christian
church teaches — then it does not wholly transcend history and
culture; rather it redeems history and culture. And redemption
is a process, sometimes a slow and gradual process.

As far as woman's civil redemption is concerned, in the
Old Testament she was still treated too often as object rather
than subject, property rather than person; but these abuses
were curbed by the laws of marriage and divorce, bondage and
freedom, property rights and inheritance. Therefore, though
such laws and customs were not perfectly just as judged by the
ideals of the Christian faith, they looked toward and prepared
for the coming of One who, as the Redeemer of all — male
and female — fully lived out the implications of the original
creation ordinance whereby human life is an "I and thou"
relationship in the specific form of male and female.

In the second place, it should be noted that in rejecting a
hierarchical model of the man/woman relationship one need
not reject all hierarchy as such. Even to suggest such a conclusion is unthinkable. Social structures would disintegrate into
anarchy and chaos were mankind to seek to live by a purely
egalitarian model of communal life. To conceive the personal
dimension as an I/thou fellowship does not imply an egalitari-

anism that knows no levels of authority and obedience, no super- and subordination in society.

In fact, in the concrete structures of life, women ought to be subordinate to men as the occasion demands. By the same token men ought to be subordinate to women as the occasion demands. It is not the subordination of *some* women to *some* men, but the subordination of *all* women to *all* men, *because they are women*, that constitutes the indefensible thesis, indeed the unscriptural thesis. When one grasps the basic contour of revelation, as it begins with the creation narratives and culminates in Jesus Christ, one cannot make a case for such ontological subordination of the female to the male.

Calvin, it will be recalled, in commenting on I Timothy 2:12, affirms that there is no absurdity in a man's obeying in one relationship and commanding in another. But this does not apply, he contends, to women "who by nature are born to obey men." This is where the argument is found wanting. Since men and women are equally in the image of God, what is true for one is true for the other. As it is no absurdity that men should obey in one relationship and command in another, neither is it that women should do so. It is best, therefore, to understand the hierarchical relations between the sexes, not in terms of the ontological, as does Calvin, but rather in terms of the *personal*. Men and women are *persons* related as partners in life. Hence *neither men nor women by nature are born to command or to obey; both are born to command in some circumstances, to obey in others. And the more personal the relationship between them, the less there is of either; the less personal the relationship between them, the more there is of both.*

This means, to give a concrete illustration, that at no time can a true marriage be likened to an army, any more than an army can be likened to a marriage. In the military enterprise, by reason of its impersonal character, hierarchy is essential.[103]

103. See the eloquent apology for hierarchy delivered by Shakespeare's Ulysses, before Agamemnon's tent, when the Greek princes addressed themselves to the question:
   Why had their high design
   To ransack Troy, within whose strong immunes
   The ravished Helen, Menelaus' queen,
   With wanton Paris sleeps,
   Dragged on these seven years? *Troilus and Cressida*, Act 1, scene 3.

Some men (and women) must command, others must obey, for an army to function. In a true marriage, by contrast, rarely will either party command or obey, and when such occasions do arise one ought not to say the husband should always give the orders because he is a man while the wife should always obey because she is a woman. Husbands are not to wives what generals are to privates. So to conceive the husband/wife relationship is to threaten marriage with tyranny on the man's part and artifice on the woman's part.[104] If one should protest that of course a husband does not "give orders" to his wife, he simply "makes the basic decisions" as head of the house, the problem remains. The general makes the "basic decisions," the private acts accordingly. The Christian marriage ceremony has traditionally required of the woman the vow of obedience, and it makes little difference whether one says she is to "obey her husband's orders" or to "accept her husband's decisions."

But if the man and the woman are partners in life, then they should share the responsibility of basic decision-making in the human enterprise. And should a particular man and a particular woman become husband and wife, they too should make the *basic* decisions jointly. When mutual agreement cannot be achieved, the husband's preference should be honored by the wife in some instances, and the wife's by the husband in other instances. Our society being what it is, it is usually the husband's preference to which the wife acquiesces in such decisions as vocation and residence. However, since the man, as husband, is not ordained to make all basic decisions nor the

104. In Molière's *École des Femmes* (Act III), Arnolphe reminds his bride-to-be that though the human race is divided into two halves, they are far from equal halves. One is the major half, the other, the minor, so that the obedience the

> Soldier displays to his appointed captain,
> The servant to his lord, the child to his father,
> The least lay brother to his Superior,
> Is nothing at all to the docility,
> And the obedience, and the humility,
> And the profound respect that a wife should show
> To her husband, who is her master, chief, and king.

What the great dramatist meant as a comedy is taken with all seriousness by many husbands on the real stage of life. Curiously, some who argue that in marriage the husband is the general, will accept women officers in the military! But the human mind is capable of many curiosities.

woman, as wife, to accept them, such decisions are not necessarily, but only customarily, the husband's to make.

As we have said, in rejecting the subordination of the woman to the man, we are not rejecting hierarchy as such, but only an expression of it that falls short of the ideal established by Christian revelation. As a matter of fact, the Christian vision of reality is hierarchical in a very fundamental way. For example, what one may call the "hierarchy of grace" in Paul's thought cannot be doubted from a Christian point of view. By the "hierarchy of grace" we mean, according to Christian doctrine, that God is the source of all authority (Rom. 11:33); that the Son of God voluntarily humbled himself as the Messiah and Savior (I Cor. 15:28), becoming obedient to his Father in all things even unto death, yea, the death of the cross (Phil. 2:6-8); that because of this obedience the Son has been highly exalted in his messianic office and made head over all things to the church (Phil. 2:9-11); and that for this reason all Christians are subject to him who is the Head, freely confessing him as Lord and Savior (Rom. 10:9). This hierarchy consisting of God, Jesus the Christ, and the Christian believer, to which Paul appeals in his argument in I Corinthians 11:3, is at the very center of Christian revelation.[105]

But the affirmation that the man is the head of the woman and the woman subject to the man is another matter. To establish this proposition the apostle used arguments with which theologians, especially in modern times, have struggled; and having established the proposition, he drew conclusions from it about the woman's role in life, especially in the life of the church, with which theologians have struggled even more. And there are reasons why they have struggled, some of which we have

105. In this regard, one might ask whether the *analogia relationis*, then, of which we spoke above (p. 36), does not imply subordination of the woman after the analogy of the subordination of the Son to the Father? The answer is no, since the subordination of the Son to the Father is not an ontological subordination in the eternal Godhead, but a voluntary act of self-humiliation on the part of the Son in the economy of redemption. As God, the Son is equal with his Father, though as Messiah he has assumed a servant role and become subordinate to his Father. The basis of the comparison between Man's being, as an "I"/"thou" fellowship of male and female, and God's being, as an "I"/"thou" fellowship of persons in the Godhead, is the doctrine of the Trinity, not the doctrine of Incarnation.

already mentioned. One of these we must now elaborate in more detail.

2. Female Subordination and the Analogy of Faith

We have rejected the argument for female subordination as being incompatible with (a) the biblical narratives of Man's creation, (b) the revelation which is given us in the life of Jesus, and (c) Paul's fundamental statement of Christian liberty in the Epistle to the Galatians. To put matters theologically, or perhaps we should say hermeneutically, the problem with the concept of female subordination is that it *breaks the analogy of faith.* The basic creation narratives imply the equality of male and female as a human fellowship reflecting the fellowship in the Godhead; and Jesus, as the perfect man who is truly in the image of God, taught such equality in his fellowship with women so that one may say — must say — that "in Christ there is no male and female." Any view which subordinates the woman to the man is not analogous to but incongruous with this fundamental teaching of both the Old and the New Testaments. To affirm that woman, by definition, is subordinate to man does not correspond to the fundamental radicals of revelation; rather it breaks the analogy of faith.

All of this, of course, is not difficult to understand. The difficulty is that Paul, who was an inspired apostle, appears to teach such female subordination in certain passages in his epistles. (It was, perhaps, for this reason that a theologian of the rank of Karl Barth felt the need to affirm it, though in doing so he lacked the conviction that former ages had brought to its defense.)[106] To resolve this difficulty, one must recognize the human as well as the divine quality of Scripture. As for the divinity of Scripture, when the theologian says that Paul was

---

106. Barth's position, though we find it unconvincing, is surely more credible than the common and facile dismissal of Paul's teaching as manifesting an obsession with the "woman problem," a symptom of some sort of sexual neurosis. As the profoundest theological mind in the apostolic age (and the most enlightened), Paul was the major interpreter of Jesus' life, death, and resurrection. Hence those who dismiss him cavalierly only commend their own thought to oblivion. Paul, as we have said, spoke the saving word, even about women, in the Epistle to the Galatians, an incomparable manifesto of Christian liberty.

"inspired" he does not mean that the apostle was a religious genius but rather that he was supernaturally guided by God's Spirit in what he taught. Indeed, behind the concept of *analogia fidei*, as an interpretive principle, is the conviction that the Spirit of God is the ultimate author of *all* Scripture. The Christian church, therefore, has rightly understood the phrase "the inspiration of Scripture" to indicate that in and through the words employed by the biblical writers God has given his word to mankind.

While the theologians have never agreed on a precise theory of inspiration, before the era of critical, historical study of the biblical documents they tended, understandably, to ignore the human side of Scripture and to think of divine inspiration in a way that ruled out the possibility of any human limitation whatever in the Bible. The Bible, for all practical purposes, was so immediately dictated by the Holy Spirit that the human writers were more secretaries than authors. Historical and critical studies of the biblical documents have compelled the church to abandon this simplistic view of the divinity of Scripture and to take into account the complexity at the human level of the historical process by which the documents were produced. Instead of the simple statement, which is essentially true, that the Bible is a divine book, we now perceive more clearly than in the past that the Bible is a divine/human book. As divine, it emits the light of revelation; as human, this light of revelation shines in and through the "dark glass" (I Cor. 13:12) of the "earthen vessels" (II Cor. 4:7) who were the authors of its content at the human level.

Keeping in mind this divine/human character of Scripture, we propose to look once more at Paul's statement of the argument for female subordination in Ephesians 5:23-33, the most familiar of all his pronouncements on the subject, as we have noted, by virtue of its use in the traditional Christian marriage ceremony. This *locus classicus*, the passage which "makes everything clear," according to Barth, is undoubtedly of prime importance in understanding the man/woman relationship. But before we turn to this task, an added word concerning the concept of the *analogia fidei* would seem to be in order.

Addendum: Analogia Fidei, a Comment

The expression *analogia fidei* appears in the Vulgate as a translation of the biblical ἀναλογία τῆς πίστεως of Romans 12:6. In modern versions this verse is usually understood to refer to the personal faith of the charismatic prophet, who is admonished to a sober use of his gift in a way that will edify the many members of the one body. He is to prophesy according to "the proportion of *his* faith." Traditionally, however, Romans 12:6 has been interpreted in a different manner. The term "faith" has been understood objectively of the teaching set forth in Scripture to which the church, as the one body of Christ, makes confession. The individual prophet who claims an inspired utterance, then, is bound by this objective norm. His utterances must correspond to, be *analogous* to, this faith of the church; he must prophesy according to the *analogy* of *the* faith.

This traditional understanding of Romans 12:6 reflects a theologico-historical point of view first clearly enunciated by Origen. According to Origen, one may speak of an "analogy of faith" because there is a likeness in the midst of unlikeness (i.e. an analogy) between the teachings of the Old and New Testaments. And since the Bible is normative for the church, whose faith is grounded in Scripture, this fundamental analogy which unites the Old and the New Testaments should not be violated in the interpretation of any given passage of Scripture as the church seeks to fulfill its teaching ministry.

Ordinarily, then, one is said to "break" the analogy of faith when one teaches something deemed contrary to Scripture. In the above argument we are using the phrase to describe what may be regarded as a disparity or incongruity within Scripture itself, namely, the inference, drawn from the rabbinic interpretation of Genesis 2, that the woman is subordinate to the man because she is derived from him, in contrast to the creation ordinance whereby Man is by definition a partnership of male and female. Our reasoning is not unlike that of Jesus — though he did not appeal to any technical hermeneutical principle — when asked how his view of divorce harmonized with the Mosaic law (Mk. 10:3-5). In this place, Jesus, in a sense, appealed to Scripture against Scripture. While he did not deny that the Mosaic law allowed for divorce, he insisted that such a law did not express the true intent of the original creation ordinance of monogamous marriage. Citing Genesis 1:27 and 2:24, he said that Deuteronomy 24:1, 3 was written "on account of the hardness of your hearts" (v. 5). In other words, the commandment in Deuteronomy reflects the cultural, historical realities of life in ancient Israel, not the will of God as originally revealed in the creation. Such reasoning, we submit, is analogous — if we may play on the word — to that which we have followed in seeking to understand the Pauline statement of sexual hierarchy in the light of the creation ordinance of sexual partnership. To say that a man may write a bill of divorce and put away his wife, or to say that the woman by definition is subordinate to the man, is to come short of the revealed intent of the Creator; it is to break the analogy of faith.

3. Female Subordination and the Bond of Marriage (Ephesians 5)

Ephesians 5:22-33, it will be recalled, stands at the beginning of the so-called Haustafel (Eph. 5:22-6:9), a series of admonitions to the several members of a Christian household. Prior to this section of the epistle Paul contrasts the old and the new life of his converts (4:17-24); lays down the rules for the new life in Christ (4:25-5:5); and admonishes his readers to walk as children of the light, being in subjection one to another in the fear of Christ (5:6-21). Then come the practical admonitions addressed to the various members of the family. From this series of admonitions it would appear that when he exhorts his converts to subject themselves to one another (5:21), he does not mean simply that in Christ everyone should be mutually submissive to his neighbor as an expression of humility. There is, in the Christian household, a certain order, and our subjection to one another in Christ is determined by this order: Wives are to be subject to their husbands as the church is subject to Christ (5:22, 23); children are to be obedient to their parents as the fifth commandment enjoins (6:1-3); and slaves are to be subject to their masters with fear and trembling, in singleness of heart as to Christ (6:5f.).

Now if one were to press the subjection of the wife to the husband in the home because of Ephesians 5:22, then he should, by parity of reasoning, press the subjection of the slave to his master because of Ephesians 6:5f. Indeed, in antebellum America, southern slave owners, as well as prominent Christian divines in both the North and South, did just that.[107] The former had the material interest of keeping their slaves in subjection, the latter added to this the theoretical interest of maintaining the authority of Paul as an inspired apostle.[108]

It is undoubtedly true that, were men enslaved without the possibility of freedom (as was the case with millions of people at the time Paul wrote), the instruction to Christian slaves to live in all integrity before the Lord — "not gainsaying, not purloining, but showing all good fidelity, so as to adorn the doctrine of God their Savior in all things" (Tit. 2:10) — would ameliorate the evil of their bondage. If, in response to the call of Christ, a slave committed himself to the Lord, the quality of his life would be humanized by the inner strength and freedom he would gain as "the Lord's freedman" (I Cor. 7:22).[109]

But the fact that Paul, in the Ephesian *Haustafel*, teaches slaves to obey their masters in the same unqualified way that he teaches children to obey their parents surely reflects the historical limitations of his Christian insight. Since God revealed himself to Israel as the Redeemer who delivered his people from the slavery of Egypt by the hand of Moses and so gave them respite from their bondage, a respite symbolized in the Sabbath rest (Deut. 5:12-15), and since this rest is fulfilled in Jesus who delivers his people from the bondage of sin, it

107. The connection between the question of slavery and women's emancipation soon became apparent to the women who took up the abolitionist cause. It was from their ranks that the first concerted plea came in America for the emancipation of women; and those who argue today for the subordination of women sound uncomfortably like those who argued for the submission of slaves a century ago.

108. Not only in Ephesians, but also in Colossians, the apostle admonishes slaves "in all things to obey their masters in the flesh" (Col. 3:22). And Titus, his assistant, is commanded to "exhort slaves to be in subjection to their own masters and to be well-pleasing to them in all things" (Tit. 2:9).

109. It is in this light that Harriet Beecher Stowe's portrayal of the ideal Christian slave (Uncle Tom) is to be understood as an authentic artistic achievement. Seen also in this light of history, one can appreciate how different in meaning were Paul's admonitions to first-century Christian slaves from the meaning given these same admonitions by early American slaveholders!

is impossible to suppose that slavery is an ordinance of God manifesting his will for the Man-to-Man relationship. To take such a position would obviously break the analogy of faith.

Since this is so, one may wonder that it was not more evident to the apostle Paul. Well, in a way it was, as can be seen from his letter to Philemon. True, he did not organize an "underground railway"; in fact he sent the runaway slave Onesimus back to his master. But he did so "no longer as a slave . . . but as a dear brother" in the confidence that "you [Philemon] will meet my wishes; I know that you will, in fact, do better than I ask" (Phm. 16, 21). This last remark is commonly understood as an oblique reference to legal manumission, cast in this indirect form because of the proprieties of polite style in letter writing, of which the apostle here shows himself a master. Such polite reserve, however, contrasts with the direct encounter Paul had with Peter over Jewish/Gentile relationships at Antioch (Gal. 2:11f.) and shows that he did not see the implications of his own great declaration that in Christ "there is neither bond nor free" as clearly as he saw the implications of his declaration that in Christ "there is neither Jew nor Greek" (Gal. 3:28).[110] But he surely saw some of the implications, or he never would have written what he did to Philemon. Who before Paul had ever said to a Roman slave master what he said? Manumission, yes. But brotherhood?

Now if the apostle's ambivalent view of the slave/master relationship reflects the historical limitations out of which he wrote the Ephesian *Haustafel*, then the same may be said of his view of the male/female relationship whereby women as such, by the Creator's intent, are subordinate to men, so that a woman, united to a man in the intimate relationship of marriage, should fear her husband, showing reverence for him as her head, even as the church, in the fear of the Lord, reverently submits to Christ her head in all things.

To admit such limitations is not to deny, Roman society being what it was, that the quality of a woman's life would be

---

110. The admonition to Christian slaves in I Cor. 7:21, ἀλλ' εἰ καὶ δύνασαι ἐλεύθερος γενέσθαι, μᾶλλον χρεῖσαι, may mean, "If a chance of liberty should come, take it." But it may well mean, "If a chance of liberty should come, choose rather to make good use of your servitude." In either case, obviously the apostle is more interested in one's spiritual status of freedom in Christ than in the social implications of this freedom.

humanized by her chaste and reverential submission to her husband, according to the apostolic admonition, especially in the light of the plain exhortation to husbands to love their wives as themselves. Nor is it to deny the "great mystery" of which Paul speaks in Ephesians 5:32, for there is indeed an analogy between the relationship of husband and wife on the one hand and Christ and the church on the other. The best statement of the analogy, however, is not in terms of Christ's lordship over the church as the Savior of the body, for obviously husbands are not lords and saviors of their wives any more than wives are lords and saviors of their husbands. Rather, the univocal element in the analogy, which helps us to grasp the mystery on which it is based, is the *henosis*, that is, the *oneness* which marks both the union between Christ and the church and between man and wife who become one flesh|(οἱ δύο εἰς σάρκα μίαν), as the apostle says in Ephesians 5:31.

But when two people become one flesh, this does not mean that the identity of the one (the wife) is absorbed into some mystical oneness with the other (the husband), but that both are conformed to a common personality, as it were, of which each partakes, in which each shares, by virtue of the marriage relationship. The common experience of marriage, to the degree that the ideal of oneness is achieved, shapes both partners so that they are congruous to each other. As the Christian must say, "For to me to live is Christ" (Phil. 1:21), acknowledging that life would not be life apart from his oneness with the Lord, so it is with husband and wife. United in the bond of marriage, each partner feels the inadequacy of a solitary existence, though obviously in a secondary, not in a primary and absolute way, as would the church apart from Christ. In both instances, then, in the covenant of grace and in the covenant of marriage, the union is maintained by a mutual love of a unique quality.[111] As we noted above, even Barth admits that

111. Whether the unique quality of this love is best described by the word *eros* or *agape* is immaterial to the analogy. The fact, however, that Scripture draws such an analogy between Christ and the church on the one side, and husband and wife on the other, may indicate that Nygren and others have stated the contrast between *agape* and *eros* too sharply. "If loving God/Is nothing like/The love I have for her — /Then you can have it." So writes poet Walter A. Kortrey, "Agape and Eros," *The Christian Century*, vol. 90, no. 27 (July 18, 1973), p. 749.

it is the mutual partnership of husband and wife which makes marriage a parable of the covenant of grace.

Those who are zealous for a divine "chain of command" in the family do not argue in our day, as in former times, that slaves are to be subject to their masters. But they often do argue that if wives were not subject to their husbands, then children would not be subject to their parents; and this would spell anarchy. Ergo, wives must be subject to their husbands. The screw that is loose in this reasoning is the failure to perceive the double meaning of the term "children." Obviously children must be subordinate to their parents until they grow up and become free persons in their own right. When this happens, though they remain children of their parents in a secondary sense, they are no longer subject to their parents as when they were children in the primary sense. Parents often fail to acknowledge that this is the case, however, and make their own and their children's lives miserable because they are unwilling to relinquish their parental rule over them.

By the same token, and perhaps even more tragically, husbands make life miserable for their wives when they treat them as children throughout marriage. Ibsen's Nora complained to Torwald in their first (and last) conversation as equals:

> You have always been so kind to me. But our home has been nothing but a playroom. I have been your doll-wife, just as at home I was papa's doll-child; and here the children have been my dolls. I thought it great fun when you played with me, just as they thought it great fun when I played with them. That is what our marriage has been, Torwald.

And when her husband reminded her that before all else she was a wife and mother:

> I don't believe that any longer, she replied. I believe that before all else I am a reasonable human being, just as you are — or — at all events — that I must try and become one.[112]

The right to be "a reasonable human being, just as you are" is a right which no woman should be asked to surrender in marriage.

---

112. Henrik Ibsen, A Doll's House, Act III, toward the end.

4. *The Magna Carta of Humanity* (*Galatians 3:28*)

Whatever limitations one may perceive in Paul's view of
the wife's subjection to her husband in all things, it cannot
be doubted that in the matter of male/female relationships as
a whole he had remarkable insights for a former Jewish rabbi.
Though he did not see all the implications clearly, he surely
grasped the essential truth that the revelation of God in Christ
radically affects one's view of the man/woman relationship. He
was the first to declare that in Christ there is no male and
female (Gal. 3:28). To contrast Paul with Jesus, then, is palpably unfair; for Jesus himself never said anything beyond
what Paul said in writing to the Galatians. Indeed, he could
not, for there is nothing more to be said: Paul's word in his
epistle of Christian liberty is the last word. We have noted
that the apostle never appeals to the first creation narrative
when speaking of the woman's submission to the man. However, in Galatians 3:28, when speaking of her equality with
the man, he does allude to this narrative. We must now look
at this significant theological affirmation more closely.

> For you are all sons of God through faith in Christ Jesus.
> For as many of you as were baptized into Christ did put
> on Christ. There can be neither Jew nor Greek, there can
> be neither bond nor free, there can be no male and female;
> for you are all one in Christ Jesus (Gal. 3:26-28).

Most versions, for the sake of symmetry, retain the "nei-
ther-nor" of the series and render the Greek in this text: "*neither* male *nor* female." Literally, however, Paul says: "No male
and female," reflecting the language of Genesis 1:27. Furthermore, the words he uses (ἄρσεν καὶ θῆλυ) are those used in the
Septuagint translation of this passage. In contrast, therefore, to
his exclusive appeal to the second creation narrative when
speaking of the woman's subordination to the man, here the
apostle clearly has in mind the first creation narrative.

Some scholars have taken Galatians 3 literally as meaning that in Christ the ordinance of creation, whereby Man is
male and female, is done away. Oneness in Christ looks toward
the final eschaton when the androgynous ideal shall be realized
and there shall be no more distinction of sexes. Such an interpretation we have rejected for reasons already given.[113] Sal-

---

113. See above, pp. 24ff., for our remarks on the androgynous ideal.

vation does not alter the ordinance of creation; rather it redeems it. Oneness in Christ cannot point in the direction of solitary Man, but only in the direction of Man-in-fellowship, for
Man-in-fellowship is the only true Man. The thought of the
apostle, then, must be that in Christ the basic divisions that have
separated Man from his neighbor, divisions which have threatened human fellowship, are done away. Not distinctions which
enrich fellowship, but divisions which destroy fellowship by
leading to hostility and exploitation — these have no more place
in Christ. The areas which the apostle mentions in Galatians
3:26-28 are race (Jew and Greek), class (slave and free), and
sex (male and female). These are bracketed together because
they have been the source of the most bitter hostility and
antagonisms; this they have in common, and from this point
of view they all stand, in the apostle's mind, over against the
new oneness or unity which is in Christ.

Yet obviously these three categories are not alike in every
respect. The distinction between slave and master is not a creation ordinance at all, but only a manifestation of Man's inhumanity to Man. It, then, is literally done away in Christ. The
distinction between Jew and Greek, on the other hand, though
hardly a creation ordinance, is consonant with creation, so long
as it is not used to foster religious exclusivism and pride.[114] It
is done away in Christ, then, only insofar as it has been the
occasion of divisions which separate Man from his fellow Man.
Paul still considered himself a Jew (albeit a fulfilled one) rather
than a Greek. As for male and female, this distinction represents, indeed, an ordinance of creation; Man has always been
and always will be male and female because God created him
so. Sexuality in a literal sense, then, is not abolished in Christ
at all. In fact it should not even be suppressed. It is not sexuality but the immemorial antagonism between the sexes, perhaps
the deepest and most subtle of all enmities, that is done away
in him. In Christ the man and the woman are redeemed from
false stereotypes, stereotypes which inhibit their true relationship. Thus redeemed, they are enabled to become what God intended them to be when he created Man in his image — a

114. Unfortunately the church has answered "Jewish" exclusivism with
"Christian" anti-Semitism, which is a denial in reverse of the thesis of
Galatians.

fellowship of male and female. The restoration of this true fellowship of the sexes is one of the ways we "put off the old man and put on the new man who is being renewed unto knowledge after the image of Christ" (Col. 3:10).

Undoubtedly, as we have noted above, in all three of these pairs — Jew/Greek, bond/free, male/female — the apostle thinks preeminently *coram Deo*, that is, in terms of the Man-to-God relationship rather than in terms of the Man-to-Man relationship. This is the truth seen by those who lay the emphasis on personal, individual, spiritual salvation as the source of renewal of all human relationships. But it is important to notice that the theological "breakthrough," if we might so speak, reflected in Galatians 3:28 had social implications even for the apostle. He saw those implications clearly enough in the first instance (Jew/Greek). Accordingly, when Peter came under the influence of certain strict and scrupulous brethren from the Jerusalem church who would not accept dinner invitations from Gentile Christians in Antioch, Paul withstood him to his face (Gal. 2:11f.). He did not say, as those from James were trying to say, that Jews and Greeks are one as to their personal salvation and enjoy a "spiritual" fellowship in Christ, but that in other respects, such as eating, things remain as they always have been — restaurants must be segregated since Jews cannot eat with Gentiles. He rather insisted on complete social integration.

In the second instance (slave/free) his vision was not so clear. Paul politely hinted to Philemon that he should set his slave Onesimus free, but he did not confront Philemon on the slave issue as he had Peter on the issue of Jews and Gentiles eating together. In a similar manner, in the great struggle for abolition in America, though it was the truth as it is in Christ which led to the abolition of slavery, churchmen for the most part did not take the lead, and many followed only from an ignominious distance. Some even defended slavery on "biblical" grounds. These spokesmen for the church emphasized the God/man relationship; they left the fight for abolition to others and concentrated on getting the souls of slaves saved. After the event, of course, the Christian community forswore all defense of slavery, though some parties in the church today, by their judicious silence, are still impeding the struggle for freedom and social justice for the disinherited.

As for the third instance in our text (male/female), here Paul was more cautious still in the implementation of his own Christian insight. He even spoke of the woman as being subordinate and unequal to the man. She must always remember that she was created for man's sake, and, as a wife, she must reverence the man who is her husband. Yet this reverence of the wife is counterbalanced by the love of the husband. Though he may not have been the first to say that a man should love his wife, the apostle gave this affirmation unprecedented depth: "A man should love his wife as himself, yea, even as Christ has loved the church" (Eph. 5:25)! How many rabbis had ever said that a man should love his wife as Yahweh loved Israel?

And the magnificent affirmation that in Christ there is no male and female (Gal. 3:28) was, for the apostle, not merely a matter of theory. He acted out this truth in a most remarkable way, for a former rabbi. He began to implement this insight, even if he did not implement it thoroughly, in his own life and in that of the church. Whereas in rabbinic usage a woman was designated only as the wife of a certain man, Paul greets women by name in the Roman congregation: Tryphaena, Tryphosa (Rom. 16:12), Julia (16:15), and Mary (16:6), commending the last for her diligent labors. Not only does he mention Priscilla (16:3) along with her husband Aquila, but he even names her before her husband.[115] In fact, the apostle, who has been maligned as a misogynist, greets by name no less than seven Christian women in Romans 16 — a cover letter carried by Phoebe, a woman whom he calls his sister and warmly commends as a servant of the church at Cenchreae (16:1-2).

As a rabbi, Paul should hardly have deigned to address a group of women when no men were present; yet he did so in Philippi without a moment's hesitation (Acts 16:13). Even less would he have acquiesced in a woman's importunate invitation to abide in her house. Yet he accepted Lydia's invitation,

115. This same Priscilla, with her husband Aquila, instructed the eloquent Apollos, a Jew "mighty in the Scriptures," in "the way of God more accurately" (Acts 18:24-26). While granting her the evident learning and ability implied by this incident, scholars have greeted with erudite indifference and condescension Harnack's suggestion that she was the author of Hebrews. They have preferred Luther's suggestion that the book was written by Apollos, her pupil!

it appears, without the slightest scruple (Acts 16:15). In all this, one can hardly fail to see how far Paul had moved in his pilgrimage from Judaism to Christianity. In fact, the letter to the church at Philippi, a church which began with the conversion and baptism of a prominent woman and her household and which met in her house (Acts 16:40), must be considered along with the letter to the church in Corinth if one is to have a balanced view of Paul's attitude toward women. If his correspondence with the Corinthian congregation reflects his Jewish background as one who had worshipped in the synagogue, his letter to the Philippians reflects a more liberalized view of the place of women in the Christian church.

While it is true that the apostle addressed this church as constituted with bishops and deacons, all of whom were males (Phil. 1:1), one can hardly reason that he simply used Lydia's conversion and hospitality as a means of establishing a bridgehead with men in the community. Women evidently played a prominent part in the Philippian church, not only at its inception, but also as it grew and developed. Two of them are mentioned by name, Euodia and Syntyche, whom Paul calls his "fellow workers, who struggled together with me (συναθλέω) in the spreading of the gospel." These the apostle exhorts "to be of the same mind in the Lord" (Phil. 4:2). Though he does not disclose the nature of their misunderstanding, his appeal to them in a general letter to the church indicates that it was not simply a private affair. Rather, the difference between them threatened the unity and well-being of the whole church. It probably related to matters of belief, worship or ethics, reflected in their views as expressed in the gathered assembly, the same assembly in which his letter would be read. Thus the apostle implies their prominence in the church and also their right to express themselves as leading members of the congregation.[116]

To the same effect is the mention by Luke of "chief women" who were prominent among the apostle's converts in Thessalonica and Beraea (Acts 17:4, 12). There must have been something about Paul's gospel and the way he expounded it which made an impact on these sensitive and gifted women. And what

116. See the provocative article by the Reverend W. Derek Thomas, "The Place of Women in the Church at Philippi," *The Expository Times*, vol. 83, no. 4 (Jan., 1972), pp. 117f.

could it have been but the profound worth which they perceived they had, as *persons*, to the Savior he preached?

We may conclude, then, that while Paul went all the way in living out the truth that in Christ there is neither Jew nor Greek, he by no means denied in his life style the implications of the further truth that in Christ there is no male and female. Here he made only a beginning, to be sure, in implementing his insight. But it is high time that the church press on to the full implementation of the apostle's vision concerning the equality of the sexes in Christ. Thus and only thus will the church become a fellowship of men and women like that which is revealed to us in the life of our Lord himself while he lived among us — too briefly — in this sinful world.

5. Conclusion

Many, no doubt, will argue, as did our forefathers in the days of the abolition of slavery, that the church should leave such social implications of the New Testament message to the civil government to implement. Let the church attend to its proper business, which is the salvation of the individual, and not meddle in controversial social issues. If enough men are converted, then women will be treated justly and with love and concern. To raise up husbands who are more loving in the home, husbands who are like the beneficent slave owners of a century ago, is what the church is commissioned to do.

Some who argue thus do so in a deliberate effort to circumvent the truth. But many who do so are sincerely concerned to be biblical; and it is true beyond all doubt that the primary concern of the church should be the God/man relationship. Those who deplore the "social gospel" have more than a grain of truth on their side; salvation with a vertical reference is the central theme of the Bible.

To such as have a sincere concern to be biblical, it may be of help to distinguish between what the New Testament *says* about the new life in Christ and the actual *degree of implementation* of this vision in the first-century church. So far as woman's role in the partnership of life is concerned, it can hardly be the degree of implementation in the New Testament church to which we should look for authoritative guidance in our present moment in history. In its implementation, the New Testament church reflects, to a considerable extent, the prevailing attitudes and practices of the times. Because of this, we should look to the passages which point beyond these first-century attitudes toward women to the ideal of the new humanity in Christ. Only thus can we harness the power of the gospel to make all history, not just first-century history, salvation history.

The example of slavery remains, perhaps, the best we have to illustrate this principle. If we believe that the abolition of slavery is the necessary implication of the message of freedom in Christ, then we cannot regard the implementation of this ideal in the New Testament church as normative. Had the church, through the centuries, interpreted "neither slave nor free" in Galatians 3:28 in terms of the explicit implementation in the New Testament, the institution of slavery would never have been abolished. The same is true of woman's liberation. The church today should not strive to maintain the status quo of church life in the first century, as though it were normative for all time. Rather, the church should seek to implement fully the principle that in Christ women are truly free. And such an effort will contribute to the liberation of all mankind, both men and women.

Speaking to this end, Sherwin Bailey makes the perceptive comment that achieving a right relationship between man and woman is a prime *desideratum* in all human affairs. God has laid upon us all, by making Man male and female, the unconditional task of living in sexual partnership. And this obligation pertains not simply to marriage, but to all the manifold variety of associations in our communal existence as men and women. We are created for each other and bound together by a tie of mutual dependence.

But in the past, this genuine partnership of mind and spirit between the man and the woman has been greatly hindered by theories of male superiority and domination. The woman has been excluded from many spheres of life, especially those where decisions are made. And her social and educational disabilities have deprived her of the means to refute the arguments by which the man has buttressed his position of privilege. The woman has had to compete with the man in a "man's world," on his terms, rather than relate to him as a partner who is equal to him in every way. In view of the many obstacles she has had to face in exercising her natural gifts as a female human being, her achievements are remarkable. Yet compared to the man's they are slight indeed. Little do we know what resources she has because of the stultifying effects of male supremacy.

In seeking a resolution to this problem, we must challenge the presumption that speaks of the "woman question." This very way of stating the matter presupposes that man's place in life has been determined and is beyond dispute. This is the first lie. If it is not good that man should be alone, if the Creator has given him a partner in life, then the "woman question" implies a "man question." The one cannot be discussed without the other. And the "man/woman" question is the question of their right relationship, a question that can never be resolved so long as one member presupposes that his role in the relationship is self-evident. *Since God created Man male and female, both must acknowledge the call of God to live creatively in a relationship of mutual trust and confidence, learning through experiment in relationship what God has ordained that they should learn in no other way. This calls for integrity on the part of the man to renounce the prerogatives, privileges, and powers which tradition has given him in the name of male headship. And it calls for courage on the part of the woman to share the burdens and responsibilities of life with the man, that in love and humility they may together fulfill their common destiny as Man.*[117]

First Addendum:
Misogyny in Western Thought

If the view of Man we have espoused is true — that God has so created Man that his very being is a being-in-fellowship — and if the fundamental form of this fellowship at the human level is the fellowship of man and woman, then any deprecation of the man by the woman or of the woman by the man is a perversion of their common humanity. The female of the

117. See Bailey, *Sexual Relation* . . . , pp. 282-284.

human species is by no means immune to this tragic propensity, but the male is undoubtedly the prime offender, the female being more the hapless victim than the miserable sinner. When one hears of an upcoming series on "The 'Woman Problem' — Then and Now" in some paper or magazine, if one has any theological insight one does not need to read the articles to know that it is really a matter of "the human problem — then and now." The male, in his selfish aggressiveness and pride toward the woman, has made her very existence and role in life a problem, not realizing that it is his attitude, not her existence, that is the fundamental problem.

Because the woman is biologically endowed to bear, nurse, and care for her offspring — a task that, until modern times, has required the best years of her life — it has been relatively easy for the male, who is physically stronger, to assign the female "her place" and keep her there. While it may be that the female would have served the male in the same manner had the situation been reversed, such an observation is neither here nor there. (Whatever "Amazons" there may have been in antiquity, besides those in the minds of Herodotus and Diodorus, the only ones in the world today are in the temple friezes and bas-reliefs of vases and sarcophagi in the museums of Europe.) The Christian view of Man is opposed to all exploitation of one's neighbor and unreservedly committed to the ideal of a humanity that is a fellowship under God of those who are made in his image.

Since men have not treated women as equals, one should not be surprised that they have rationalized their action by theorizing that women are somehow inferior in their humanity and hence do not need to be treated as equals. Misogyny has taken different forms, but it is a recurring theme throughout the history of Western thought.

Scholars sometimes dwell on the noble ideal of woman in classical Greek antiquity, naming the immortals of Greek poetry — Helen, Penelope, Andromache, Antigone, Kassandra— but the remarks of Pseudo-Demosthenes (59, 112) tell the real story of woman's life in ancient Greece:

We have harlots for our pleasure, concubines for daily

physical use, wives to bring up legitimate children and to be faithful stewards in household matters.[118]

After Achilles slew Hector outside the gates of Troy and celebrated the funeral of Patroclus, the Achaean warriors engaged in various contests for prizes which Achilles, son of Peleus, offered them.

> The son of Peleus now brought out the prizes for the third contest and showed them to the Argives. These were for the painful art of wrestling. For the winner there was a great tripod ready for setting upon the fire, and the Achaeans valued it among themselves at twelve oxen. For the loser he brought out a woman skilled in all manner of arts and they valued her at four oxen. He rose and said among the Argives, "Stand forward, you who will essay this context."[119]

Whereupon mighty Ajax and crafty Ulysses struggled valiantly till "their backbones cracked — and sweat rained from them in torrents," to win, not a woman, but something more prized than a woman — a "tripod ready for setting on the fire."

Homer's *Iliad*, in which this scene occurs, begins what Robert Hutchins has aptly called "The Great Conversation." It is Volume IV in the *Great Books* series, a series setting forth the fundamental ideas that have shaped Western civilization from Homer to Freud. Seventy-three authors carry on this "great conversation," and there is not one woman among them to speak on anything whatsoever. Women are more silent in this conversation than in any of Paul's churches. And when it comes to the subject of woman, it is some conversation! Indeed, it would be difficult to find a theme on which greater minds have expressed meaner thoughts.

Plato (*Timaeus*), having told us how God implanted immortal souls in bodies, observes that he who lives an evil life will, upon reincarnation, pass into a woman. Aristotle, the father of biology, in his treatises on the *History of Animals* and the *Generation of Animals*, repeatedly treats the female as a kind of defective male ("the female is, as it were, a mutilated male," *The Generation of Animals*, II, 3, 3) — a piece of pseu-

118. Quoted in Oepke, "γυνή," TDNT, I, p. 778.
119. *Iliad*, VIII, 273. *Great Books*, IV, p. 168.

doscience which Thomas Aquinas found not wholly incompatible with Christian theology.

But it is not simply in ancient paganism that such blatant misogyny is found. Some of the greatest minds of modern times have articulated similar miserable vulgarities. Philosophers like Schopenhauer and Nietzsche have constructed elaborate portraits of woman's inferiority. To Schopenhauer women were "childish, frivolous, and short-sighted and existed solely for the propagation of the species." Nietzsche inveighed against their "pedantry, superficiality, presumption, petty licentiousness and immodesty," and thought that a man who believed they were equal to himself was a "shallow" man. Charles Darwin found women constitutionally inferior in everything "requiring deep thought, reason or imagination, or merely the use of the senses or the hands," which would appear to say it all.

But it remained for Sigmund Freud, in the name of the science of psychology, to explain in what sense Aristotle's "mutilated male," who is a "female," is really mutilated. She lacks a penis, and the envy which this anatomical deficiency has created in her is the key to the woman's psychosexual life. And her sexual life is the key, in turn, to understanding woman. This crude bit of misogyny is set forth in Freud's *New Introductory Lectures on Psychoanalysis*. Lecture 33 is devoted to "The Psychology of Women," a lecture, he assures us, that not only serves as an example of the detailed work of Analysis, but may be commended for two specific reasons: "It contains nothing but observed facts, with hardly any speculative additions, and it is concerned with a theme which claims your attention almost more than any other."

"Throughout the ages," Freud informs his audience, "the riddle of woman has puzzled people of every sort. . . . You too will have pondered over this question insofar as you are men; from the women among you that is not to be expected, for you yourselves are the riddle."

Betty Friedan, who seems at times to have some of the same awe for Freud's accomplishments in psychology as St. Thomas had for Aristotle's in biology, yet complains:

> The fact is that to Freud, even more than to the magazine editor on Madison Avenue today, women were a strange,

inferior, less-than-human species. He saw them as child-like dolls, who existed in terms only of man's love, to love man and serve his needs. It was the same kind of unconscious solipsism that made man for many centuries see the sun only as a bright object that revolved around the earth. Freud grew up with this attitude built in by his culture — not only the culture of Victorian Europe, but that Jewish culture in which men said the daily prayer: "I thank Thee, Lord, that Thou hast not created me a woman," and women prayed in submission: "I thank Thee, Lord, that Thou hast created me according to Thy will."[120]

She notes Freud's derision for John Stuart Mill's views on female emancipation and the analogy Mill saw between the suppression of women and of Negroes. Reviewing Freud's views on female psychology, she asks:

What was he really reporting? If one interprets "penis envy" as other Freudian concepts have been reinterpreted, in the light of our new knowledge that what Freud believed to be biological was often a cultural reaction, one sees simply that Victorian culture gave women many reasons to envy men: the same conditions, in fact, that the feminists fought against. If a woman, who was denied the freedom, the status and the pleasure that men enjoyed, wished secretly that she could have these things, in the shorthand of the dream, she might wish herself a man and see herself with that one thing which made men unequivocally different — the penis.

She would, of course, have to learn to keep her envy, her anger hidden: to play the child, the doll, the toy, for her destiny depended on charming men. But underneath, it might still fester, sickening her for love. If she secretly despised herself, and envied man for all she was not, she might go through the motions of love, or even feel slavish adoration, but would she be capable of free and joyous love? You cannot explain away woman's envy of man, or her contempt for herself, as a mere refusal to accept her sexual deformity, unless you think that a woman, by nature, is a being inferior to man. Then, of course, her wish to be equal is neurotic. . . .

120. Betty Friedan, *The Feminine Mystique* (New York: Norton, 1963), p. 108.

Because Freud's followers could see woman only in the image defined by Freud — inferior, childish, helpless, with no possibility of happiness unless she adjusted to being man's passive object — they wanted to help women find sexual fulfillment as women, by affirming their natural inferiority.[121]

"Thus," she complains, "Freud's popularizers embedded his core of unrecognized traditional prejudice against women ever deeper in pseudoscientific cement." Instead of throwing Freud's book away, they threw it at their female patients. In this way, American women were driven back into the home, where they did not need an education and where, in the place of freedom and rights as human beings, they could have security and fulfillment as women.

The feminine mystique, elevated by Freudian theory into a scientific religion, sounded a single, overprotective, life-restricting, future-denying note for women. Girls who grew up playing baseball, mastering geometry — almost independent enough, almost resourceful enough, to meet the problems of the fission-fusion era — were told by the most advanced thinkers of our time to go back to the doll's house by Victorian prejudice. And their own respect and awe for the authority of science — anthropology, sociology, psychology share that authority now — kept them from questioning the feminine mystique.[122]

Not only Western thought in general, but Christian thought in particular, has been disgraced by an unworthy prejudice against woman. Woman, declaims Chrysostom, is "a necessary evil, a natural temptation, a desirable calamity, a domestic peril, a painted ill."[123] Speaking of these and other contemptuous epithets with which the Fathers of the church loaded the name of woman, D. S. Bailey observes that many of them reflect failings of females which were due to the disabilities they suffered in ancient times; yet certain alleged moral defects in the female character cannot be so explained.

She is to be suspected and avoided as a subtle and dangerous temptress, always inclined to beguile man and to inflame

121. Friedan, *The Feminine Mystique*, pp. 117-119.
122. Friedan, *The Feminine Mystique*, p. 125.
123. As quoted by Kathleen Bliss, *The Service and Status of Women in the Churches* (London: S.C.M. Press, 1952), p. 17, n. 1.

him with evil passions. Hence the injunction of the Fathers against cosmetics and every kind of adornment and dress, on the ground that they are calculated to excite lust in the beholder; men must be protected against the wiles of the sirens who would ensnare them, and draw them into the ways of immorality. Nor is it enough for woman to eschew these artificial aids to enticement; "even natural beauty," writes Tertullian, "ought to be obliterated by concealment and neglect, since it is dangerous to those who look upon it." In church she must be veiled, lest by uncovering her face she should invite another to sin, while she should avoid banquets, marriage feasts, the bath, and all other places where her presence and charms might stimulate the desires of men.[124]

The great Ambrose of Milan, whose preaching of Christ moved the young Augustine to godly tears, must have provoked tears of another sort in his female parishioners when he accused them of impeaching the handiwork of the Creator by their ill-advised efforts in self-beautification.

> The Lord says, "Thou canst not make one hair white or black"; and dost thou wish to have greater power so as to bring to nought the words of the Lord? With rash and sacrilegious hand thou wouldst fain change the colour of thy hair: I would that, with a prophetic look to the future, thou shouldst dye it the colour of flame . . . .[125]

A millennium of Christian history did not relieve the image of woman the temptress. Novella d'Andrea, A.D. 1312-1366, one of the few learned women admitted to a chair in the venerable University of Bologna, lectured on philosophy and law behind a curtain lest her face should distract the students. Even down to modern times this theme has persisted and is occasionally repeated in some disquisition against women preachers.

In the traditional thought of the theologians, this sinister fascination of the female, by which she had beguiled mighty men like Samson and spilled the blood of holy men like John the Baptist, was grounded in the primal history of the race. Eve, who was created second, sinned first. Hence she and all

---

124. Bailey, *Sexual Relations*, with sources from Athanasius, Clement of Alexandria, *et al.*
125. As quoted in Philip Schaff, *Church History*, V, p. 566.

her daughters belonged to the guilty sex that caused Man to be expelled from the Paradise of God. This was her crowning offense.

> "Do you not know," thunders Tertullian, "that each of you is also an Eve? . . . You are the devil's gateway, you are the unsealer of that forbidden tree, you are the first deserter of the divine law, you are the one who persuaded him whom the devil was too weak to attack. How easily you destroyed man, the image of God! Because of the death which you brought upon us, even the Son of God had to die. . . ."[126]

On the basis of the biblical narrative of the fall, woman has been branded as the ultimate cause of Man's ills. As in ancient Greek mythology Pandora opened the fateful box, so in Christian thought it was Eve, the first woman, who ruined mankind. This interpretation of the fall narrative was inherited by Christian thinkers from the Jewish rabbis who had used it to keep the woman in a subservient role to the man. "Desire did not dare," disclaims Philo, "to apply its deceitful art of temptation to the man; but it perverted the woman and through her the man. . . . The woman since the fall into sin must bear heavy burdens; also the loss of freedom, and dependence on her husband, whose command she must obey."[127]

This caricature of the woman as the ruin of the man reaches its apogee in the medieval theory of witchcraft, the alleged malevolent magic of women who had made a compact with the devil. There were occasional male witches (wizards) in medieval Christian Europe, but the woman was supposed to be the almost exclusive repository of magical powers to destroy, powers with which she was invested by the devil. Though the New Testament mentions the Lord's saving grace in the life of Mary Magdalene out of whom came seven demons (Lu. 8:8), and Paul's deliverance of the unfortunate damsel with a python spirit (a deliverance which threatened her male exploiters, Acts 16:16-19), there is no such redemptive note to be heard

126. De cult. fem. 1.1, as quoted in Bailey, Sexual Relation . . . , p. 64.
127. As quoted in Leipoldt, Die Frau . . . , p. 66. In Roman Catholic theology, to be sure, this defamation of Eve's memory is countered by heaping praise upon Mary. Male theologians, however, might better identify with Eve in her guilt than bestow encomiums on Mary for her submission to heaven's design.

in the fulminations of churchmen against the abominable practice of witchcraft.

This is not to imply that witchcraft was the invention of Christian misogynists (it is found in pre-Christian cultures), nor to deny that the demonic element in moral evil is a legitimate theological concern. But in medieval Europe the deplorable suspicion of the female character, inherited from the Fathers and fused with elements of folklore and superstition, betrayed the church into some of the most atrocious cruelties ever perpetrated by humans on their fellow humans.

On December 7, 1484, Pope Innocent VIII promulgated the bull *Summis desiderantes* in answer to questions from German inquisitors. It has been said that of all the documents ever issued from Rome, imperial or papal, this one cost the greatest shedding of innocent blood. Rather than use the papal authority to deny or at least question the credibility of the evidence for witchcraft, Innocent assumed the evidence to be incontrovertible. Indeed the leading scholars of the church, from St. Thomas on down, accepted the cohabitation of humans, especially women, with demons. (Nor did any Protestant Reformer utter a word against the theory. Luther, in fact, expressed the opinion that those who pursue the dark arts deserve to burn.) In 1486 the *Witches' Hammer* (*Malleus maleficarum*), the "most portentous monument of superstition the world has produced," was issued by the Dominican inquisitors. A manual for detecting and prosecuting witches, it went through numerous editions (13 before the year 1520) and amassed evidence extracted from thousands of witnesses, chiefly women. Crazed by the agony of torture, these hapless creatures confessed everything that imagination could suggest. According to this infamous manual, the work of highly educated men, the bewitched were transported through the air to so-called "witches' sabbaths" where they consorted with the devil and lesser demons, indulged every vice, and were instructed in all sorts of fell arts. By these they afflicted men and beasts alike. Husbands could not beget, nor wives conceive or bring to birth. The fruits of vine and orchard were blighted as hailstorms and tempests were raised.

Of all the parts of the *Witches' Hammer*, none is so infamous as the authors' vile estimate of woman. The very title,

Malleus maleficarum, is in the feminine because, as the authors inform their readers, the overwhelming majority of those involved in this hellish conspiracy are women. They even derive the Latin word for woman, *femina,* from *fe* and *minus,* that is, *fides minus,* "less in faith." Deceit is the very essence of woman's nature; she deceives because she was formed from Adam's rib, and that was crooked.[128] A long chapter is devoted to women's inferiority to men, and their alliance with demons is dwelt upon with apparent relish. The authors, Heinrich Institoris and Jacob Sprenger, German Dominicans, thank God they are men and indicate that few of their sex consent to such obscene relations because of the male's natural vigor of mind. Helen, Jezebel, and Cleopatra are cited as exemplifying that pernicious agency which has wrought the destruction of whole kingdoms. And the words of Jesus ben Sirach are frequently cited: "Woman is more bitter than death."

It was believed that old women, especially, could inflict an evil essence upon the young by a glance of the eye. Multitudes of these women were pierced with pins and needles in an attempt to detect a spot where the blood would not flow. Such a spot was considered indicative of a demonic spell. The condemnation and punishment of such women in batches was not uncommon.

Pico della Mirandola declared that one might as well deny the discovery of America as doubt the existence of witches. Richard Baxter, the irenic peacemaker, applauded some of the worst cruelties in England, as did Cotton Mather in New England. As late as 1768, John Wesley declared that "giving up witchcraft was giving up the Bible."

The only voices lifted against the superstition became themselves the victims of the mania they deplored. One such unfortunate was the burgomaster of Bamberg, Germany, who still speaks in a letter to his daughter written in 1628 from his prison cell.

> Many hundred good nights, dearly beloved daughter, Veronica. Innocent have I come into prison, innocent must I die. For whoever comes into a witchprison must become a witch or be tortured till he invents something out of his

128. Recently a woman named Margaret Sitter Ermath has set this part of the record straight by entitling her book on women in the church, *Adam's Fractured Rib* (Philadelphia: Fortress Press, 1970).

head and — God pity him — bethinks himself of something. I will tell you how it has gone with me. . . . Then came the executioner and put the thumb-screws on me, both hands bound together, so that blood ran out at the nails and everywhere, with the result that for four weeks I could not use my hands, as you can see from this writing. . . . Then they stripped me, bound my hands behind my back and drew me up. I thought heaven and earth were at an end. Eight times did they do this and let me drop again so that I suffered terrible agony. [There follows a rehearsal of the confessions he was induced to make.]

Now, dear child, you have all my confessions for which I must die. They are lies made up: All this I was forced to say through fear of the rack, for they never leave off the tortures till one confesses something. . . . Dear child, keep this letter secret so that people may not find it or else I shall be tortured most piteously and the jailers be beheaded. . . . I have taken several days to write this for my hands are both lame.

Good night, for your father, Johannes Junius, will never see you more.

Here, indeed, a man has spoken — since the vast multitude of women who suffered like fate were all but illiterate, having been denied learning as well as life. Had *they* written of *their* trials and tribulations, as did Junius, who could endure the pathos? These pitiable creatures did not have before them the prospect of a martyr's crown nor the glory of a heavenly bliss. They were not buoyed up by the sympathy and prayers of the church. Held in horror by those who had been nearest and sometimes dearest to them, subject to the indignity of having the hair shaved from their bodies and especially from their secret parts, lest some imp or charm be hidden there, they were whipped, banished, and burned at the stake. And thus, unpitied and unprayed for, writhing on the rack till they confessed, they yielded to the cold scrutiny of the inquisitor and the consuming power of the flames.[129]

129. Of many sources, one may consult A. D. White, *History of the Warfare of Science with Theology in Christendom;* and Philip Schaff, *History of the Christian Church,* vol. VI, sec. 59, "Witchcraft and Its Punishments," pp. 514-532. The letter of Johannes Junius is translated in this latter source, pp. 531-532.

Second Addendum:
The Ordination of Women

1. Introduction

While one can hardly do justice in an addendum to the question of women and the Christian ministry, yet, inasmuch as we have argued that our humanity is given us as a *fellowship* of male and female, and inasmuch as we believe the church to be a fellowship, a *communio sanctorum*, it is only fitting that we should make a brief statement at this juncture summarizing the traditional reasons for refusing ordination to women and offering a brief response in terms of the theology of Man as male and female which we have espoused.

Those who would deny women full access to the sacred office of the ministry have argued that there are some deep and significant reasons "in the very nature of things" why men, and only men, should be ministers in the church of Christ. These reasons, whether elaborated in a Roman Catholic or in a Protestant frame of reference, finally reduce to three: the nature of woman, the nature of the ministerial office, and the nature of God himself.

2. The Ordination of Women and the Nature of Woman

Serious debate over women's right to the holy office of the Christian ministry is a relatively modern phenomenon, its having been assumed — more or less — throughout Christian history that women should not be admitted to the ranks of the ordained clergy for the obvious reason that they participate in the general limitations of womanhood.[130] At its meanest, this assumption has been little more than an instance of the misogyny rehearsed in the previous addendum, a prejudice which occasionally can still be read between the lines of the ongoing discussion, though it is no longer an explicit part of the argument against the ordination of women.

Carefully avoiding all demeaning aspersions against the woman, there are those, still, who protest the erotic stimulus

130. For the exceptions to this rule see Joan Morris, *The Lady Was a Bishop* (New York: Macmillan, 1973).

aroused in the male by the female presence. They are careful, of course, to state that this is a matter of male weakness, not female perversity. Mascall, for example, quotes with approval the argument of Williams that "men as such are very less likely to be an involuntary cause of distraction to women, under the circumstances of public worship, than women are to men; and that this is a permanent fact of human nature which can no more be abolished by modern progress than the law of gravitation can be abolished by human progress."[131] The trouble with this argument is that it proves too much. As Mascall admits, pressed to its logical conclusion, it would exclude women from all visible, official participation in worship and, unless the senses of sight and sound are fundamentally different, would appear to exclude them from participation even in an invisible choir, a restriction even more stringent than the limitations imposed by Eastern Orthodox and Roman Catholic communions.

In truth, the argument that females should not be ministers and priests because males have a "weakness" is an argument bankrupt of all merit. It is simply a disarming nuance of the age-old assumption on man's part that the woman is a sex object; that she differs from the man in that while he is *capable* of erotic love, she is *made* for it. As Byron wrote,

> Man's love is of man's life a thing apart;
> 'Tis woman's whole existence.

It is this very attitude that has made it so difficult for the woman to transcend the erotic, even in a religious situation.[132] There-

131. E. L. Mascall, *Women and the Priesthood of the Church* (London: Church Literature Association, no date, pp. 8-9), quoted from the address of N. P. Williams delivered at the Convocation of Canterbury, June 1938. For a Baptist statement of the same argument, see Herbert Carson, *Reformation Today*, no. 5 (Spring, 1971), p. 9: "If a man stands in the pulpit the average woman is not unduly affected by his appearance; but if a woman stands there, men, being men, will often find that their thoughts are less on the word spoken than on the speaker."

132. *Variety Magazine* called Aimee Semple McPherson, preacher of the Foursquare Gospel, "sexy but Episcopalian, an angel with an oblique Mona Lisa smile." When she preached in England, the *London Daily Mail* commented on her short skirts, flesh-colored stockings, and elaborate coiffure, sometimes Titian-red, sometimes blond, always her own. Asked by reporters years later, after her "kidnapping," if she intended to marry again, she replied: "My life will always be for Jesus." See Ishbeh Ross, *Charmers and Cranks* (New York: Harper and Row, 1965), pp. 252ff. This last remark about living only "for Jesus" reminds one of the eroticism found in

fore, rather than limiting the woman in her freedom as a child of God by denying her calling to the ministry on such grounds, men ought to redeem the man/woman relationship in the church by repenting of their sin.

3. The Ordination of Women and the Nature of the Ministerial Office

In the debate over the woman's right to the office of ministry, the question of the nature of woman always leads into the further question of the meaning of ordination. This is necessarily so, inasmuch as every major ecclesiastical tradition — Eastern Orthodox, Roman Catholic, and Protestant — recognizes that there is an office of ministry and that ordination is the way one is inducted into it. Hence ordination, however one may conceive it, is (usually) necessary if one is to function as a minister in Christ's church with the authority of one divinely called to the task. Since one is "called of God" to the office, one does not simply choose to be a minister as one would choose to enter a profession. One must be called and the call must be confirmed by the church. The question, then, is whether God calls women, as he does men, to be ministers in his name. Those who oppose the ordination of women answer in the negative. And they rebut the charge that such an answer is obscurantist, in that emancipated women have excelled in all other professions, by pointing out that the ministry cannot be equated simpliciter with a profession like law or medicine.

But granting this worthy and needed clarification, we can hardly accept this as the final word on the subject. The question then must be asked, "Why should God call only men; why should he not also call women?" To this question it has been answered that what the husband is to the bride, Christ is to the church. Hence the one vested with authority to minister

---

female religious mystics throughout the ages. Catherine of Siena (1347-80), perhaps the greatest of them all, was given a wedding ring by Jesus which was the ring of flesh cut off at his circumcision. In St. Theresa's famous vision where a golden dart is plunged into her heart, "I am certain," she testifies, "that the pain penetrated my deepest entrails and it seems as if they were torn when my spiritual spouse withdrew the arrow with which he had penetrated them." As cited in Simone de Beauvoir, The Second Sex (New York: Knopf, 1968), pp. 632-633, 636.

in his name must be one whom God has appointed to function in the church as does the husband who, at the natural level, is the head of the family. In other words, to ordain a woman to holy orders would be analogous to assigning her the role of husband and father in the family, a role which properly belongs to the man. We see, then, that so far as the nature of the min- isterial office bears on the question of woman's ordination, the ultimate issue proves to be her relationship of subordination to the man.

This is true regardless of one's specific theological view of ordination. It really matters little whether one has a Catholic view of ordination wherein the essential element is the sacra- mental commissioning of a priest to pronounce absolution and celebrate the sacrifice of the Mass, or whether one has a Protes- tant and evangelical view wherein the essential element is the setting apart of a minister to preach the gospel and shepherd the flock of God. In both traditions it is the woman's relation- ship to the man that disqualifies her for ordination. We make this statement fully aware of the frequent disclaimers to the contrary. And, admittedly, there are other considerations, to which we shall address ourselves presently. But so far as the *nature of ordination* is concerned, those who object to giving it to women always come, in the last analysis, to the same place: the Christian minister is Christ's representative, and this implies a spiritual authority in the church that belongs to the man. The question of female ordination, then, is a nuance of the larger question of female subordination.[133]

133. St. Thomas plainly stated the impossibility of female orders in terms of the woman's deficiency in spiritual receptivity and power. Be- cause the apostle said a woman cannot teach or use authority over a man, it is therefore "not possible in the female sex to signify eminence of degree, for a woman is in a state of subjection. It follows that she cannot receive the sacrament of orders." Thomas therefore concludes that ordi- nation without a *male* person is like Extreme Unction without a *sick* person. He lists female sexuality as impediment number one to receiving holy orders, followed by such impediments in the male as defectiveness of reason, the state of servitude, the guilt of homicide, the stigma of illegitimacy, and the condition of physical mutilation. (See his *Summa Theologica*, Supplement 29, 1.) Contemporary thinkers who stand in the Neo-Thomistic and Anglo-Catholic traditions speak not of the *inferiority of* the woman to the man, but rather of her *difference from* him, especially as this difference is reflected in her role as wife and mother in the natural family, a difference which must be reflected in the church as the spiritual family of God.

At this stage of the discussion, it is no secret what the present writer thinks of the whole idea of female subordination. It remains only to translate the view that Man in the divine image is a partnership of male and female into the language of ecclesiology. So translated, that view may be expressed as follows: *the church is a universal priesthood of all believers in Christ, female as well as male.* To this affirmation it has been answered that such references as I Peter 2:5, in which Christians generally are called a "holy" or "royal priesthood," refer to the priesthood communicated to the church *in its corporate aspect.* Hence the priesthood of *all* believers implies nothing for the ordination of women to holy office unless one adopts the radical laicism implied in that form of Protestantism which admits of no *essential* difference between laity and clergy.

Although this writer is a Protestant in this radical sense, he is not convinced that such an answer is valid even from a Roman or Anglo-Catholic perspective, since according to the Catholic view, "priestly character," committed individually by ordination to those who function as priests in the church, arises directly out of the priestly character which is committed generally to the church as Christ's body. But if this is so, if individual priesthood rests upon the general priesthood of the laity, then women, who, like men, are incorporated by baptism into the body of Christ and so made "to be priests unto his God and Father" (Rev. 1:6), are equally qualified to become priests in the individualized meaning of the term. Whatever difference one may postulate between the priesthood in its general and in its individual form, this difference implies *nothing* for men that it does not imply for women.[134] In fact, since the church is the bride of Christ and therefore feminine to him, one could just as well reason that the universal priesthood of all believers should find its individual expression in the woman *rather than* in the man, an inference which the theologians, as males, have never drawn.

134. The same reasoning applies *mutatis mutandis* to the consecration of women to episcopal office, since all who are made priests in Christ are also made "kings" or "a kingdom" (Rev. 1:6). All this being the case, the fact that women were ordained as Baptist ministers before they were ordained as Presbyterian ministers, and that they will be ordained as Episcopal priests before they will be ordained as Episcopal bishops, and that they will be ordained as Episcopal bishops before they will be ordained as Catholic priests, is historically interesting but theologically insignificant.

4. The Ordination of Women and the Nature of God

Since our extensive analysis of the man/woman relationship has centered about the concept of the *imago Dei*, the reader will sense that when we come at last to the question of the nature of God, we have arrived at the crucial and fundamental theological issue insofar as the ordination of women is concerned. All theological questions are questions about God, and the question "Whom may the church rightfully ordain?" is no exception.

As we have observed in the course of our previous discussion, the *analogia relationis* — whereby the fellowship of Man as male and female may be compared to that of God as Father, Son, and Spirit — is not to be pressed so as to suppose a sexual distinction in God. Theologians have always known and admitted as much, yet they have hardly been consistent in applying this truth. While they have assumed that God is not female, it has been less clear to them that he is not male either. While their own bias as men has been a factor in this lack of perception, there are, no doubt, more substantive reasons for the general tendency of theologians to think of God as a male Deity. Scripture uses the masculine pronouns in speaking of God, and this God, who reveals *himself* in Scripture, is the *Father* who sent his *Son* to redeem mankind; and this *Son* became incarnate as the *man* Jesus of Nazareth.

Surely it is understandable — if not defensible — that theologians should have inferred from all this that God is more like the male than the female of the human species. Though herself a bearer of the divine image, the woman does not bear that image to the same degree as the man. She is, as it were, one degree removed from that original; she is the "glory of the man" who is the "image and glory of God" (I Cor. 11:7). By the same token, it is surely understandable that Christian women have struggled with the implications of their faith at this point. Theresa of Avila's bitter lament, "The very thought that I am a woman is enough to make my wings droop," has struck a responsive cord in many, and today's women theological students have turned the saint's lament into a complaint that they find the male Deity of the theologians more oppressive than redemptive.

Those who reject the claim of women that the church

should confirm their call to the ministry and invest them with the authority of office through ordination have pointed out that the teaching that God is the "Father," who sent his "Son" to be our Redeemer, rests on *revelation*, not human invention. C. S. Lewis sharpens the issue by asking a series of rhetorical questions: Can one say that we might just as well pray to "Our Mother who art in heaven" as to "Our Father"? Dare we suggest that the Incarnation might just as well have taken a female as a male form and that the second person of the Trinity might just as well be called "Daughter" as "Son"? Can we reverse the mystical marriage so that the church is the "Bridegroom" and Christ the "Bride"? All this, Lewis avers, is involved in the claim that a woman can stand in the place of God as does an ordained minister. Hence, to admit women to the office of the ministry would for Lewis and those who share his views be to turn Christianity into a different sort of religion.[135]

These profound mysteries of God's being, mysteries revealed in the Incarnation, explain (allegedly) why our Lord, himself a man, restricted the personal exercise of the ministry in his church to apostles who were men. Being God's eternal *Son*, he became a *man*, not a *woman*; and for this reason he commissioned *men*, not *women*, to represent him in the church, which is his body, his bride. In fact, the Gospels testify more clearly to Jesus' institution of the ministry than to his institution of the church. He founded the church, one could say, by founding the ministry. Hence the church is built upon the foundation of the apostles and prophets, Christ Jesus himself being the chief cornerstone (Eph. 2:20). It is from this perspective, also, that we must understand the controversial pronouncements of Peter and Paul, leading apostles, to the intent that women should keep silent in the church and not aspire to the teaching office. And because all this is so plain in the New Testament, the *onus probandi* lies with those who would simply set aside the ecclesiastical tradition, whereby the ministry has been entrusted to men, as mere tradition having no authority in the church today.

Though we cannot respond fully to this argument in this place, we must offer some response, for it is incompatible with our foregoing conclusion that human sexuality is a life partner-

135. See his essay "Priestesses in the Church?", reprinted in *God in the Dock* (Grand Rapids, Mich.: Eerdmans, 1970), pp. 234f.

ship of equals under God. Obviously there can be no true partnership and equality of the sexes in the life of the church so
long as those vested with the authority to speak for God are
men and men only. Our response will take the form of a series
of brief affirmations as follows.

a. If, as the theologians have taught, there is only a personal distinction in God (Trinity), not a sexual one, then the
creation of Man in the divine image as male *and* female can
hardly mean that Man is like God as male *rather than* female.
Since God is a fellowship of persons (Father, Son, Spirit) and
Man is a fellowship of persons (man and woman), therefore
Man is like God as man in fellowship with woman, not as
man in distinction from woman.

b. Such a conclusion, which appears to be beyond dispute,
requires that we construe the masculine language about God
analogically, not literally, when we interpret Scripture. The
univocal element in the analogy is the *personal*, not the *sexual*,
meaning of the language.

c. Related data of Scripture, when carefully examined,
support this conclusion. Even in the Old Testament, where
God reveals himself to Israel as like a *Father* (Mal. 1:6; 2:10),
he also reveals himself as like a *Mother*: "Can a woman forget
her sucking child that she should have no compassion on the
son of her womb? Yea, she may forget, yet will I not forget
you" (Is. 49:15). The fact that God likens himself to a Father
much more frequently than to a Mother does not alter the
analogical character of the paternal, as well as the maternal,
language of such Scriptures.[136]

When we turn to the New Testament, the same situation
prevails. Jesus likens God to an anxious shepherd who rejoices
when *he* finds a lost sheep (Lu. 15:3-7) and to an anxious

136. Speaking of the infrequency in the Old Testament of maternal
usage with reference to God, it is not as infrequent as might be supposed.
For example, the unfaithfulness of Israel is rebuked in the line of the
Deuteronomist, "You were unmindful of the Rock that bore you, and you
forgot the God who gave you birth" (Deut. 32:18). While the first verb
יֶלֶד may mean "beget," its common connotation is "bear." The second
verb חֹל, to "writhe" or "twist" (in the pain of childbirth), can only be
maternal. Hence to translate, "You were unmindful of the Rock that begot
you, and you forgot the God who *fathered* you" (*New Jerusalem Bible*) is
indefensible. It imposes male imagery on female usage, a translation
procedure which has incurred increasing feminist protest.

woman who rejoices when *she* finds a lost coin (Lu. 15:8-10). Such male and female analogies are equally revelatory because Man is like God as male *and* female.[137]

d. Because the language of the Bible about God is analogical, the personal pronouns used of God — he, his, him, himself — in Scripture, theology, and devotion, are to be understood *generically*, not specifically. Though such *personal* pronouns are necessary because God is not the philosophic Absolute or Ground of Being (Tillich) but the God who reveals himself as personal Subject (*I* am who *I* am, Ex. 3:14), it is just as wrong to understand these personal pronouns as masculine as it would be to use feminine or neuter pronouns. God is no more (or less) "he" specifically than "she," no more (or less) like the male than like the female.

e. Since the trinitarian fellowship of the Godhead knows no distinction of male and female and since the human fellowship of male and female knows no discrimination against the female as less in the divine image than the male, therefore the Incarnation in the form of male humanity, though historically and culturally necessary, was not *theologically* necessary.

To the argument that God must have known what he was doing when he became incarnate as a man, the answer may be given that indeed he did! And what exactly was he doing? He was entering into the stream of human life, and this life had a history. God was crossing the line, coming from *beyond* time and place into *our* time and place. Hence he could not ignore the actualities of the human historical situation.[138] But this is just to say that there is no ultimate reason, either in the nature of Man the creature or of God the Creator, but only a proximate one in history — and that a history marked by sin and alienation — that God should uniquely reveal himself in a man rather than a woman. The faith of the Christian, to be sure,

137. In this regard it should also be noted that whereas a yearling *male* lamb or goat answers in type to Jesus, our Passover, sacrificed for us (Ex. 12:5-6; I Cor. 5:7), yet our Lord likened himself to a *hen* who gathers her chicks under her wings (Mt. 23:27). Likewise Paul, who likens himself to a *father* who begot the Corinthians through the gospel (I Cor. 4:15), also likens himself to a *nurse* who cherishes her children (I Thess. 2:7) and to a *woman* in travail. laboring to bring children (in this case, the Galatians) to the birth (Gal. 4:19).

138. See Leonard Hodgson, "Theological Objections to the Ordination of Women," *Expository Times*, 77 (1965-66), pp. 210-213.

acknowledges that Jesus, a first-century Jew, is Lord. But this confession implies not that salvation is of the male but of the Lord. This is the meaning of the confession that makes one a Christian.

As the Incarnation cannot be understood apart from the actualities of the historical situation in which it occurred, so it is also with the male constitution of the original apostolate. Though in Christ there is no male and female, the apostles whom our Lord commissioned had to preach in a world that knew male and female in terms of headship and submission. While our Lord's intent, through the preaching of the apostles, was to redeem mankind and so create a new humanity in which the traditional antagonisms of the sexes would be reconciled, such redemption could not be accomplished by simple confrontation. One can understand, then, why he chose only men to herald the truth of the gospel in the Greco-Roman world of the first century. But one should no more infer from this fact that the Christian ministry must remain masculine to perpetuity than one should infer from the fact that the apostles were all Jews, that the ministry must remain Jewish to perpetuity.

f. Congruent with this last consideration is the fact that the New Testament itself points beyond this limitation of an all-male apostolate, and it does so in a remarkable way when one considers the times and circumstances in which the church was born. Here we have in mind such considerations as the following. (1) According to the fourfold Gospel tradition the risen Christ first appeared to women and commissioned them to tell his brethren. Hence women were the initial witnesses to the event which is at the heart of the apostolic message and the basis of all Christian kerygma.[139] (2) Women shared in the Pentecostal effusion of the Spirit. Hence there is no reason to suppose that they observed a discreet silence when the church was born, since Peter himself quotes Joel: "I will pour out my Spirit on all flesh, and your sons *and your daughters shall prophesy*" (Acts 2:17). Reinforcing this account is the statement that

139. Renan (following Celsus), in his *Vie de Jesus*, singles out Mary Magdalene as the unstable female who perpetrates the idle tale of the resurrection on the world. As a typical male chauvinist he comments disparagingly: "The passion of an hallucinated woman gave to the world a risen God!" As quoted by Philip Schaff, *History of the Christian Church* (Grand Rapids: Eerdmans, 1955), I, p. 179, note 1.

the daughters of Philip exercised the prophetic gift (Acts 21:9), as well as the statement that women prophesied even in the Pauline churches (I Cor. 11:5). Further, as the same apostle says, the church is built upon the foundation of the apostles and prophets (Eph. 2:20), some of whom, it would appear, were women. In other words, the essential qualifications and gifts which men brought to the office of ministry in the New Testament, women also brought. (3) Paul speaks of Euodia and Syntyche of the Philippian church as they who "labored with me in the gospel" (Phil. 4:3), using the graphic verb συναθλίζω; he greets Priscilla in Rome as a fellow worker (συνεργός, Rom. 16:3) and commends Phoebe, the bearer of the Roman epistle, as a helper (προστάτις) of many, whose business in the capital city warranted the support of all the saints (Rom. 16:1).[140]

5. Conclusion

In the light of these considerations, we conclude that women have full title to the order of Christian ministry as God shall call them. Let those who scruple only consider what it has cost the church not to use the talents of the woman. Let anyone consult the hymnbook and see what women poets — Fanny Crosby, Charlotte Elliott, Frances Havergale, Christina Rossetti, Anne Steel — have taught the people of God to sing and then ask what it would mean if such women were allowed to move beyond the relative anonymity of the hymnal to the full visibility men have had in the church as evangelists, preachers, and teachers. And let all who would help them attain such visibility remember that sharing the ministry with women does not mean requiring them to think, speak, and act like men. This would be to misunderstand the meaning of our sexual complementarity. Because God made Man male and female, in the natural realm men are fathers and brothers, while women are mothers and sisters. So it must be in the spiritual realm. And when it is, then, and only then, will the church be truly the *family* of God.

140. In this passage, προστάτις, literally "a woman set over others," should hardly be taken to mean that Phoebe was a woman "ruler." Rather the meaning would seem to be that she was one who cared for the affairs of others by aiding them with her resources. But such a description goes far beyond the Dorcas image implied by the translation often found in contemporary versions of this passage, "I commend unto you Phoebe, a deaconess. . . . "

IV

Epilogue: The Ontology of Sex
(The Eternal Feminine)

We have probed the question of Man's being as male and female in an effort to contribute to a more adequate theology of sexuality. In the course of the discussion we have rejected the traditional view which affirms the headship of the man, as the bearer of the image and glory of God. According to this view, the woman, who is the glory of the man because taken from him and created for him, is the man's helpmeet, especially in procreation through her function as wife and mother. By contrast, we have opted for a theology of sexuality in which the man and the woman are partners, mutually complementing each other in all the relationships of life, including marriage.

Since the Creator has given us our humanity as a fellowship of male and female, it is only as we achieve the ideal of partnership that we achieve the ideal of humanity. And this partnership is not simply an abstract "ideal," but a concrete reality, since God in Christ has actually begun the creation of a new humanity in which there is no male and female. The historic rivalry between the sexes which has characterized fallen human history, a rivalry in which the man has subjugated the woman, treating her as an inferior, and in which the woman has taken her subtle revenge, is done away in Christ. Admittedly, in a sinful world this new humanity remains a future hope as well as a present reality; yet it is a hope which the church should strive to realize ever more perfectly here and now.

It might appear anomalous in the extreme that in such a discussion we have given so little attention to the ontological question: What does it mean to *be* a man or a woman? If our very existence is an existence in the fellowship of male and

171

female, what is the ultimate nature of this polarity? Sexuality permeates one's individual being to its very depth; it conditions every facet of one's life as a person. As the self is always aware of itself as an "I," so this "I" is always aware of itself as *himself* or *herself*. Our self-knowledge is indissolubly bound up not simply with our *human* being but with our *sexual* being. At the human level there is no "I and thou" *per se*, but only the "I" who is male or female confronting the "thou," the "other," who is also male or female. What, then, does it mean to say: I *am* a male? I *am* a female? What *is* a man? What *is* a woman?

D. S. Bailey, recalling the deep sleep which came upon Adam when Eve was created, observes that there is a divine secret here, a secret about our being which has never been disclosed. The intuitive awareness that one is a man or a woman does not convey an understanding of its meaning.

> Thus sex remains a profound and baffling enigma of personal existence, the mystery of which can never be dispelled by excogitation — and certainly not by studying what is now both popularly and scientifically called "sex," or by venturing upon casual venereal experiments.

This, says Bailey, is perhaps the most unpalatable of all truths to an age which thinks it knows "all about sex."[1]

The admission that there is something about human sexuality which is the Creator's secret, that in this matter the divine word has been, as it were, sealed up, is a commendable emphasis found more in contemporary than in traditional theological thought. Not that theology puts a premium on ignorance, but theology is best done in humility. Barth, as we have observed, though he writes voluminously on the subject of the relationship between the sexes, eschews all definitions of man and woman as such. The man and the woman are alike, he tells

---

1. Bailey, *Sexual Relation* . . . , pp. 280-281. The lexical usage of the biblical creation narratives, of course, is not to be discounted. In the first narrative, "male and female" translates זכר ונקבה (Gen. 1:27), two words of obscure origin which appear to derive from roots denoting respectively "the sharp one" (one with a penis) and "the perforated one" (one with a vagina). In the second narrative (Gen. 2:18-23), where we read of the "deep sleep" that fell upon Adam, "man" and "woman" translate איש and אשה, from roots denoting respectively "the strong one," and "the delicate one." While the etymology of these Hebrew terms reflects the primal data of experience, obviously it contributes little to our understanding of the ultimate meaning of sexual polarity.

us, yet different, and this difference is as mysterious as it is obvious. The biblical account of Man's creation, he is careful to say, does not disclose to us the ultimate nature of our dual being as male and female.

Emil Brunner comes eventually to the same conclusion, if a bit more indirectly. While he ventures the opinion that our sexuality is a penultimate, not an ultimate, aspect of our humanity, something which we have in common with the animals, yet he believes that this animal sexuality in our case is caught up into the psychical and spiritual elements of human personality so as to be transformed into something quite beyond mere animal instinct. Our sexuality penetrates to the deepest metaphysical ground of our personality. As a result, the physical differences between the man and the woman are a parable of psychical and spiritual differences of a more ultimate nature.

When, however, Brunner ventures to describe these ultimate differences — woman's nature is more "receptive," man's more "productive"; woman's more "introverted," man's more "outgoing"; woman's more "conservative," man's more "inquisitive"; woman's more given to "preservation," man's to "generation"; woman's to "cultivating," man's to "establishing" — he immediately has to add that there are women who are *exceptions* to this rule, so that the difference between the sexes becomes increasingly obscure as we leave the physical realm. While our individuality is a sexual individuality, women have good cause, he admits, to suspect that our contemporary understanding of this phenomenon has more to do with sanctified tradition than with the divine creation ordinance. His final word is that no more crucial problem confronts the theologian today, as he seeks to frame a doctrine of Man, than that of sex.[2]

This humility on the part of the theologians is due in some measure, no doubt, to the complexity of the question. Even at the elementary level of biology, where it is easiest to state what a man *is* in distinction to a woman and what a woman *is* in distinction to a man, the situation is by no means simple. Scientists today distinguish as many as five biological variables, ranging all the way from chromosomal factors in the cell nucleus to the external genitalia, all of which are usually congruent in male and female human beings. But the very multiplicity of these

2. *Das Gebot und die Ordnungen*, p. 358.

factors and their possible incongruity at the individual level (as when a woman who is a well-adjusted female in society has an XY chromatin pattern so that every cell in her body is male!) gives a hint at how complex sexual definition can be even in the realm of greatest objectivity.

And this is only the beginning of our understanding of human sexuality. Over and beyond chromosomes, gonads, hormones, and genitalia is the whole realm of sexual identity, an identity which empirical research is showing to be in large measure a matter of psychological and social conditioning. This is not to say that the idea of biological inheritance, involving modes of behavior differing in males and females, is to be rejected like the "ether" of the physicists. There are, indeed, male and female instincts, maternal and paternal instincts, at the human level as at the animal level. And our sexuality as humans has much to do with our instincts.

But unlike the animals, Man actualizes these instincts by a very elaborate process of learning. For this reason, when a *scientific* answer — with which the theologian must reckon — is sought to the questions, "What *is* a man?" "What *is* a woman?", increasingly we are aware of how misleading a purely biological approach can be. Our anatomy is not our destiny. We must go beyond biology to psychology and sociology. And as we do so, as we understand more of how the human psyche develops toward maturity, we understand more of the process by which biological males and females acquire and maintain their respective masculine and feminine identities in society.

As a result of such understanding it is apparent that much of what was traditionally deemed "natural" for boys and girls, as they grow up and become men and women, is really learned behavior. Though it is still as true as it ever was that people are sexually different from birth — and this is the biological given corresponding to the theological affirmation that God created Man male and female — yet it is also true that as soon as parents determine how one shall be reared, whether as a boy or as a girl, a very complex learning experience begins which results in one's becoming a man or a woman. Furthermore, parents rear a child as a boy or girl largely according to the mores of a given society. Hence individuals gain their sense of identity, including their sexual identity as masculine or feminine persons, within a cultural frame of reference that assigns different roles to men than to women. Though it is true that the fathers who beget are always men and the mothers who bear are always women, yet in many ways one's role varies as a function of one's culture.[3] It is this ability of the human species to interchange fundamental cultural functions that humbles many of our traditional theological pronouncements, especially about woman, since these pronouncements confuse roles in a given society with the ordinance of creation. Hence theologians have felt constrained to acknowledge what Helmut Thielicke has called the "phenomenology" of human sexuality, an area in which one finds amazing plasticity.[4] In other words, the questions, "What *is* a man?" "What *is* a woman?", can no more be resolved by a psychological or sociological determinism than by a biological determinism. With the advance of technology, even physical differences of muscular strength and menstrual cycles have become increasingly irrelevant as a basis for assigning roles in society. And when men and women are given equal educational opportunities, supposed differences of intellectual capacity vanish altogether.

Yet male theologians have been slow to perceive the implications of all this. As Aquinas (and others) traditionally brought to their understanding of man and woman discredited biological perspectives, so now some theologians reflect the same mistake in the use they make of psychology and sociology. The result is that when they probe the nature of sexuality, they lapse into the traditional stereotypes. Arguing, for example, that in the erotic encounter the self is formed from beyond itself, Thielicke goes on to conclude that woman reveals more of her essential personhood in the sexual encounter than does the man. This, supposedly, is because she is identified with her sexuality quite differently from the man. It is her "vocation" to be a lover, a companion, and mother. Therefore, even in the career woman who sublimates them, these fundamental characteristics remain discernible as the sustaining powers of her calling.

3. Here the research of anthropologist Margaret Mead comes immediately to mind. See her *Sex and Temperament in Three Primitive Societies* (New York: Morrow, 1935).

4. See Helmut Thielicke, *Theologische Ethik*, III, Erster Excurs, "Die Plastizitat des Menschlichen Sexualverhaltens" (Tübingen: J.C.B. Mohr [Paul Siebeck], 1958), pp. 554f.

The man, on the other hand, invests much less of himself in the sexual relationship. He has tasks and aims which carry him beyond his sexuality to confront what Schiller describes as the hostile forces of life. Man is the one who struggles, ventures, schemes, hunts. In fact, the very physiological structure of the sex organs is not without significance, according to Thielicke. Whereas the woman receives something to herself in the sex act, the man discharges something from himself — frees himself, as it were, from it. This unusually forceful symbolism can hardly be set aside. Given this perspective, Thielicke goes on to explain (not to justify) the male tendency toward polygamy and the double moral standard.[5] Actually such erudite analysis of the nature of human sexuality is unworthy of the name "Christian." It is simply more of the incurable effort to understand the female in terms of the male, an effort which is at least as old as the Greeks and as ill-fated as the biology of Aristotle.[6]

The empirical evidence of Man's capacity to interchange sexual roles in different cultures not only challenges traditional stereotypes but is consonant with the basic theological affirmation that Man is given his humanity in such a way that he must confirm himself in it. As a free, self-transcendent subject, that is, as the bearer of the *imago Dei*, Man receives his humanity not simply as his nature but as his responsibility. And this responsibility is grounded in an ineluctable relationship to God and one's neighbor, a relationship which makes Man's very being a being-in-decision. This freedom in fellowship, which marks Man's existence in the divine image, points up the problem of seeking an ultimate understanding of Man's sexual being, his maleness and femaleness, in terms of the traditional roles assigned to men and women in a given culture. And why so?

5. See Thielicke, *Theologische Ethik*, III, "Die Verwirklichung der Gerschlechtsnature," pp. 572f. A condensed version of this argument appeared in *The Christian Century* under the title: "Realization of the Sex Nature" (Jan. 15, 1964), p. 73.

6. As we have long known that the woman is not restricted to nourishing a preformed individual, so it now appears that the egg does not simply await the seeking, penetrating sperm. Rather it is active in conditioning the sperm in anticipation of a final union in which both are transcended in a new beginning. Not that the male sperm is simply a reagent, but neither is it superior to the female egg. Biologically speaking, in procreation there is complete complementarity of the sexes.

Because women have not enjoyed the same freedom as men in choosing their roles in any culture.

Perhaps because they vaguely perceive that this is so, some astute thinkers have had recourse to the asylum of ignorance, especially as far as *woman's* nature is concerned. Kierkegaard, for example, looked upon womanhood as something so complicated, strange and confused that only a woman could live with the contradiction.[7] Simone de Beauvoir, animadverting on this female "mystery" so dear to the masculine mind, observes that it permits the man to find an easy explanation for all that appears so inexplicable in women. Thus he can avoid admitting his ignorance. He can go on maintaining a negative relationship to the woman rather than relating to her authentically as a human being. The woman, hidden behind her veil, is for the man both angel and demon, one whose fundamental being is marked by ambiguity. Mlle de Beauvoir admits that the deepest enigma in our humanity, the bond in each person between the bodily and the psychic life, is accentuated in the woman — this, because of the very complexity of her physiology.[8] But in a truly perceptive paragraph, she illumines the heart of the matter, which is not the woman's physiology but the man's ego, his inflated opinion of himself.

> Surely woman is, in a sense, mysterious, "mysterious as is all the world," according to Maeterlinck. Each is subject only for himself; each can grasp in immanence only him-

7. In attributing to Kierkegaard this view of woman, expressed, *passim*, in his *Stages on the Road to Life*, it is acknowledged that in the pseudonymous writings not all the opinions are Kierkegaard's. But this one surely seems to be.

8. Mlle de Beauvoir believes the physiological factor accounts for the fact that the woman has never been able to achieve an equal share in life with the man. Because of the demands made upon her in propagating the species, it has been relatively easy for the man, through custom, tradition, mores, and legal status, to suppress the woman and frustrate her transcendence as a person. Of course the man compensates her for her submission, as would any lord his vassal, with protection and with moral and economic justification. Thus the woman is induced, as a rule, to evade the risks of freedom by which one becomes truly human. She is lulled, as it were, into taking the easy road through life, avoiding the strain involved in authentic existence (*The Second Sex*, Introduction, xiiiff.). One is reminded, in this regard, of several American "feminist" movements which encourage women *ad nauseum* to idolize the golden chains by which they are kept in a subordinate position to men. See, for example, Helen B. Andelin, *Fascinating Womanhood* (Santa Barbara: Pacific Press, 1971).

self, alone: from this point of view the *other* is always a
mystery. However, to men's eyes the opacity of the self-
knowing self, of the *pour-soi*, is denser in the *other feminine*; men are unable to penetrate her special experience
through any working of sympathy; they are condemned to
ignorance of the quality of woman's erotic pleasure, the
discomfort of menstruation, and the pains of childbirth.
The truth is that there is mystery on both sides: as the
other who is of masculine sex, every man, also, has within
him a presence, an inner self impenetrable to woman; she
in turn is in ignorance of the male's erotic feeling. But in
accordance with the universal rule I have stated, the categories in which men think of the world are established *from
their point of view, as absolute: They misconceive reciprocity, here as everywhere.* A mystery for man, woman is
considered to be mysterious in essence.[9]

Christian theology — unfortunately — has not escaped this
error of "misconceiving reciprocity." The theologians have
sought, like the philosophers, to understand the woman in
terms of the man rather than to understand Man as a fellowship, a reciprocity, of male and female. Having defined the man
in small letters as the primary instance of Man in capital letters,
theologians have then sought to understand woman from this
masculine point of view. This is just another way of saying
that traditionally theologians have answered the question, "What
is a woman?", in a way they have never answered it about themselves. The woman's *raison d'être* lies outside herself in the
man, but this is not reciprocally true for the man. The *raison
d'être* of *his* existence lies in God, not in the woman. The man
is not created for the woman, but the woman for the man.
However, if what has been said above is true, if Man is the one
who has his being in the fellowship of male and female, then
such a one-sided approach to the question of his being is bound
to yield the wrong answers.

In the light of all this, it should come as no surprise that
some, at least, among contemporary theologians are not so sure
that they know what it means to *be* a man in distinction to a
woman or a woman in distinction to a man. It is because the
writer shares this uncertainty that he has skirted the question
of ontology in this study. Whether or not the entire effort to

9. Beauvoir, *The Second Sex*, pp. 240-241. Italics added.

deal with sexual polarity in theological categories is a *cul-de-sac,* surely much of the traditional effort has proven to be so.

As an illustration of the problem, we shall conclude this epilogue with a brief review and analysis of what may be called the classical attempt to understand the meaning of human sexuality in theological terms: the concept of the Eternal Feminine.

The expression "Eternal Feminine" has been used to mean everything that supposedly characterizes the nature of woman, whether it be divine or demonic or some admixture of both.[10] It would be a waste of time to pursue these speculations in detail. We are rather concerned here with the concept as it has been used by the theologians of the church, especially in the Roman Catholic tradition.[11] The "Eternal Feminine," even as a legitimate theological theme, does not rest on any direct exegetical base in Scripture; it is rather an inference appealing especially to those who are given to a somewhat mystical approach to Christian dogma. The fundamental assumption behind this inference — which we would not dispute — is that the empirical world contains symbols whereby we apprehend, as it were in a mirror, ultimate spiritual Reality. Specifically, the sexual polarity which characterizes our life as human reveals to us something of the mystery of God's own being and of our relationship to him.

Though not generally elaborated, there is an "Eternal Masculine" implicit in the thought of the "Eternal Feminine." Willi Moll, for example, appealing to the dogma of the Trinity, seeks to understand the masculine in our humanity as a reflection of the Father and the Son, whereas the feminine is a reflection of the Spirit. The Father, in the generation of the Son, and the Son, with the Father in the spiration of the Spirit, are both

10. Betty Friedan, in a penetrating exposé, has subsumed this indeterminate conglomeration of male arrogance under the general caption: *The Feminine Mystique.*

11. Many Roman Catholics, of course, like many Protestants, use the term "Eternal Feminine" in a very loose way to refer to all aspects of the woman question. See, for example, George Gordon Coulton, *Five Centuries of Religion,* IV (Cambridge: Cambridge Univ. Press, 1923-1950), ch. 59, which is entitled: "The Eternal Feminine." This chapter is simply an historical account of the struggle of religious reformers to keep monks from having any contact with women. Rather than "The Eternal Feminine," it might better have been entitled: "The Eternal Masculine (Battle)."

active. So, at the creaturely level, is the man. Hence he is the
direct image of God. But the Spirit is passive, the One who
receives his being from the Father and the Son. So, at the
creaturely level, is the woman, who receives her being from the
man (Adam) and is thus also in the image of God. And as
the Spirit is anonymous in the Godhead, so is the woman in
the created order. Hence her symbol is the veil.[12]

It is especially in the drama of the Incarnation that those
who seek to frame a theology of the Eternal Feminine have discovered the materials needed for the task. The relation of the
eternal Son to the virgin mother, and the respective roles of
mother and Son in the work of salvation, are deemed revelatory
of the Eternal Masculine and the Eternal Feminine in their
mutual polarity and complementarity. The following summary
of the Eternal Feminine will reflect this incarnational perspective.

In the phrase "Eternal Feminine," the adjective "eternal"
means that woman is being understood, not in the light of biological, psychological, sociological, and historical considerations,
but *sub specie aeternitatis*. Assuming that the created world
mirrors the eternal world, the thought is that the woman, as empirical bearer of the feminine principle, uniquely symbolizes the
theological mystery that our "strength is made perfect in weakness" (I Cor. 12:9). Openness to the unsearchable counsel of
the Almighty, surrender to his will rather than reliance on our
own strength, is the essence of the religious experience of mankind. This is Man's *summum bonum*, the meaning of his existence as the creature who lives, moves, and has his being in God.

For the Roman Catholic there is one person in whom this
metaphysical mystery of our humanity has become supremely
tangible and hence intelligible. That person is a woman named
Mary who became the virgin mother of our Lord. The dogmas
that cluster about Mary constitute the most significant pronouncements ever made about woman. Her immaculate conception, for example, reveals the countenance of the creature be-

12. Moll elaborates these views in two works: *Father and Fatherhood*
(Notre Dame: Fides, 1966) and *The Christian Image of Women* (Notre
Dame: Fides, 1967). Such theologians speak of the "anonymity" of the third
person of the Trinity because the term "spirit" is both the generic word to
describe God's being (God is spirit) and the specific designation of, or
trinitarian name for, the third person of the Godhead.

fore the fall.[13] This is why the larger responsibility is shouldered by Eve in the biblical story of the fall. Woman was tempted, not as the weaker member, but as the one to whom belongs the ascendency in the original creation. Mary's perpetual virginity, to mention another dogma, is the expression of the inviolable purity required in the creature who would strive for noblest achievement. Here male life intersects with female life at the empirical level in such well-known cases as celibate priests or soldiers who devote themselves to virginity in the pursuit of some ultimate goal.[14]

But it is supremely in Mary's response to the angel's annunciation that we see surrender to God as the only absolute power which the creature possesses. In her words, "Behold, the handmaid of the Lord; be it unto me according to thy word" (Ecce ancilla Domini, fiat mihi secundum verbum tuum, Lu. 1:38), we have revealed the essence of all religious experience, the cooperation of the creature in the work of salvation by an act of self-surrender. This, then, is the ultimate meaning of femininity: openness to the Divine, self-surrender in humility to God and so to one's neighbor.[15]

Traditionally appeal has been made to the role of woman

13. The definition of the dogma of the Immaculate Conception is contained in the Bull, Ineffabilis Deus, promulgated by Pius IX, Dec. 8, 1954. The Virgin's sinlessness is affirmed in Canon 23 of the Council of Trent, A.D. 1545-63; and as early as the First Lateran Council under Martin I, A.D. 649, Canon 3, there is reference to "the holy and ever virgin and immaculate Mary. . . . "

14. The dogmatic definition of Mary's perpetual virginity is promulgated in Canon 3 of the First Lateran, A.D. 649: "If any does not acknowledge . . . that Mary, as really and truly the Mother of God (θεοτόκος), . . . without loss of integrity brought him forth and after his birth preserved her virginity inviolate, let him be anathema."

15. "Through the Annunciation," says the Angelic Doctor, "the consent of the Virgin given in place of the whole human race was awaited." Summa Theol., III, Q. 30, a. 1. In the subsequent dogmatic development of this pivotal theme, the essential form emerges complete in Leo XIII's encyclical Octobri Mense, 1891: "We may . . . affirm that we can receive absolutely nothing from the great treasury of all grace which the Lord has brought forth, . . . nothing, unless God so willing, it is bestowed on us through Mary. So that, just as no one can have access to the Father most high, except through the Son, so, in almost the same way, no one can have access to the Son except through the Mother." The final evolution of this theme is the dogma of the Bodily Assumption contained in the Apostolic Constitution, Munificentissimus Deus, promulgated by Pius XII, Nov. 1, 1950.

in history as confirming the meaning of femininity defined in Marian dogma. Woman, it is pointed out, has not had the determinative voice of the man in shaping human history; she is not endowed with the historically effective talents of the man. Rather she is the silent carrier of those powers by which mankind shapes his destiny.[16] While the man expends his strength, the woman transmits it. The man exhausts himself in his own immediate work; the woman gives away her strength to those who come after her. In the man the focus is on the individual; in the woman, on the larger group. He signifies the eternal value of the moment; she, the unending sequence of the generations. The woman, then, passes on her talent; she is the one through whom the great forces of life and history proceed, though she remains nameless, concealed behind the veil, the symbol of surrender and self-effacement.

The woman does, indeed, come to the fore in history: in time of need she emerges in the field of objective achievement. When the man cannot meet the demands made upon him, the woman "comes to the rescue." To use a familiar example, when the male seed fails, the daughter substitutes in the line of succession, even assuming the royal authority. But strictly speaking, such activity is not activity but surrender, a nuance of the woman's *fiat mihi*. As in the case of the biblical Deborah, a charismatic vocation is evident whenever a woman attains the ultimate heights of achievement. It is no accident, therefore, that the greatest feminine genius is manifest in the religious sphere. No woman in the secular realm could surpass the greatness achieved by a Hildegard von Bingen, a Joan of Arc, a Catherine of Siena. It is this factor of charisma which has enabled the man, the exclusive bearer of the church's hierarchy, to recognize such specifically feminine achievement as authentic. Charisma does not imply power to produce in one's own strength but rather obliteration of the self to the point of becoming simply the instrument of God in the moment. Hence the lives of the great women of history disclose the inner meaning of creaturely cooperation as they follow the path that Mary trod. And so we see that such charismatic achievement is veiled

16. This is the theological statement of the Mother's Day sermon theme: "Behind the hand that wields the sceptre is the hand that rocks the cradle."

achievement, achievement entirely within the boundaries of the feminine.

In Mary, to return to the prototype of the eternal woman, we see every stage of the fulfillment of the feminine mystery. She is literally virgin, bride, and mother at one and the same time. And the concern of every Christian woman is to reproduce this eternal image in her own life. The virgin must absorb the concept of spiritual bride and mother, while the bride and mother must return again and again to spiritual virginity.

As for the virgin (*virgo*), too often it is naively supposed that the unmarried state is one of expectancy only, a state that may end in a negative, the disappointment of the bachelor or spinster. In the teaching of the church, in contrast to such a mistaken view, a supreme value is placed on Mary as the *perpetual* virgin. In this dogma the church expresses for all time the truth that virginity has its place of dignity alongside motherhood. Those religious, therefore, who take a vow of celibacy (priests and nuns), being overshadowed by the Spirit, accept the *fiat mihi* of Mary and devote themselves in the unmarried state to the same mystery signified in marriage, namely, the mystery of charity. In such an act of self-denial we perceive that the individual has value only as he exists before God. From this perspective a shaft of light descends through all the levels of solitude which mark the virginal existence.

Such a religious dialectic, of course, is at cross-purposes with worldly reasoning, since the contemplative life stresses the fact that Man's final destiny is in God, not in his achievement in the world. While the life of the unmarried woman from the perspective of the world appears solitary and unfulfilled, in reality it has transcendent and ultimate meaning. It echoes the avowed surrender of the creature and symbolizes the renunciation of all worldly achievement.

As for the bride (*sponsa*), the litany of the marriage ceremony, the nuptial Mass, speaks of the polarity between the masculine and the feminine as the mystery by which the generations of the human race are created and continued. In this relationship, on which all life depends, the woman's role as the bride is one of cooperation with the man. The nuptial mystery is first of all not that of the mother but that of the bride. To be a bride is not simply the first step to motherhood, any more than to be a virgin is the first step to marriage. The bride is an independent bearer of the feminine mystery. Hers is one of the three timeless aspects of the Eternal Feminine. As Mary's marriage was childless, so the church accepts the childless marriage as entirely valid and indissoluble.

In this cooperative, life-long response of the bride to the man who loves her as his wife, an eternal light falls on the secular sphere of creative companionship between the sexes. As friend and fellow-worker, the woman is the spouse of the masculine spirit; the Beatrice, as it were, of Dante; the Victoria Colonna of Michelangelo; the Frau von Stein of Goethe. Occasionally the woman in this relationship herself creates, as did Elizabeth Barrett Browning. But generally woman's part is merged into the creative work of the man in an attitude of self-giving and surrender. (The bride receives her name from the groom; Beatrice is veiled as she approaches Dante.) This aspect of the Eternal Feminine is exemplified in the great religious orders. St. Francis and his followers, for example, in a spirit of love and poverty confronted a culture which was smothered in luxury with the ideal of renunciation of worldly goods in absolute surrender of the self to God, an ideal which exemplifies the feminine mystery. Hence even at the historical level such religious orders have always had their female counterpart. In like manner, following the footsteps of woman, who is the nameless one, the master builders of the great cathedrals preserved their anonymity and did their work to the glory of God alone.

Those who believe in the Eternal Feminine congratulate the feminist movement on gaining a foothold in those fields traditionally served by men. Woman can point with pride and gratitude to the way in which she has supplemented man's work as teacher, physician, lawyer, social worker, and scholar. But her progress becomes a tragedy when she presses her rights in a way that is dissonant with her feminine nature, as when she repudiates her place in the home and family. Her emancipation can never be found in the renunciation of marriage. Woman can assert her womanly quality only as the carrier of the womanly symbol, the veil, the sign of her espousal. The cultural role of woman, inherent in the eternal orders, is that of bride to the masculine spirit, the spirit of the man. Otherwise the man/

woman relationship is degraded. In this degradation the woman becomes both devotee and victim of the most miserable of all cults, the cult of the female body. Thus she tears asunder the bonds connecting her with her metaphysical destiny; she becomes the scarlet woman of the Apocalypse (Rev. 17).

As for the mother (*mater*), it is in this role that woman finds her natural fulfillment. One can only rejoice in the benefits of modern medicine which have palliated the pain of childbirth; but one should not yield to the temptation, latent in technology, to interfere with the awesome primal powers revealed in the woman as the carrier of life. (Those who think in terms of the Eternal Feminine are not a little suspicious of contraception and abortion.) In motherhood woman supremely exemplifies self-sacrifice. Motherhood involves not only giving birth, but protecting that which is born. To be "motherly" means to give oneself unreservedly to the weak and helpless. In this embracing of weakness we stand close to the border of the world beyond this world. She who protects the little ones shares in the blessing which is theirs as the heirs of the kingdom of heaven.

And so it is through the woman, and supremely through the blessed virgin Mary, that salvation comes to mankind. Hence woman's role will always reflect the maternal. Even in the most masculine of professions, politics, a woman rules not as a man but as a queen mother. Not only does England remember its Queen Bess, and Austria its motherly empress Maria Theresa, but Lombardy still recalls its good Queen Theodolinde.

In her role as mother, the woman is closely linked with the church, which is feminine in its essence. The church, as the "Mother" of us all, symbolizes the principle of cooperation with him who works within her, Jesus, the Son of Mary and the Son of God. For this reason the church could never entrust the priesthood to women, for to do so would destroy, in symbol, the timeless significance of the woman in her intimate relationship to the inner life of the church. In Roman Catholic theology, Paul's word to the Corinthian women that they should not speak in the church cannot be construed in terms of prevailing custom alone. It is a matter not of underrating the woman, but of recognizing that in the apostolate of silence she represents the hidden life of Christ in his church.

As a bearer of this mission the woman is a true daughter of Mary. The reproduction of this image of womanhood (virgin, bride, mother) is possible for the individual woman only as she is willing to assume the attitude of the handmaid of the Lord, only as she is ready to surrender herself wholly to God. More is involved, of course, than the salvation of the woman *per se*; her salvation points beyond itself. Its proper realization is mankind's appointed mission. Mary's work signifies not only the salvation of woman but the salvation *through* women of all mankind. Woman's mission, then, reaches far beyond the woman as such, and touches the ultimate mystery of the world — the response of the creature to the Creator.

For the believer in the Eternal Feminine, therefore, woman is understood not simply as woman but as woman placed in an order of life ordained by God. To disregard woman's symbolic significance, to fail to understand her insofar as her countenance is metaphysical, is to disregard the *fiat mihi* and thereby the religious element of human life as a whole. Usually such a misunderstanding results from the self-assertive pride of the man, but it may also be a consequence of the woman's denial of her own symbol. Both are a repudiation of the Eternal Feminine. When this happens, the world becomes a man's world, in the evil sense represented by the four horsemen of the Apocalypse (Rev. 6:1-8). Such a world without woman is really a world without God, a world in which Man depends on human strength alone. Such a world is self-destructive, since Man can be truly Man only in the spirit of the *fiat mihi* of the virgin. Only when met by the religious power of a ready openness, the "be it unto me" of the woman, can the Divine Power, breaking in from heaven, renew the earth to the glory of God.[17]

17. In the above summary, we have followed in the main the argument elaborated by Gertrude von le Fort in *Das Ewige Frau*. This highly significant study by a German baroness and convert to Roman Catholicism, published in 1934, sold over one hundred thousand copies in the original German and has been translated into many languages, including English, under the title, *The Eternal Woman* (Milwaukee: Bruce, 1962). Charlotte von Kirchbaum responded to le Fort in her *Die Wirkliche Frau* (Zurich: Evangelischer Verlag, 1949), which has not been translated. In this response, Fräulein von Kirchbaum gives special attention to the question of Mariology and its refutation. In the above synopsis, in the interest of framing the argument for the Eternal Feminine in as ecumenical a form as possible, we have chosen not to enlarge upon this aspect of the discussion.

In evaluating the merits of this argument the fundamental issue is not the Marian dogma of the Roman Catholic Church. One could reject that dogma, as the present writer does, and still accept the thesis of the Eternal Feminine.[18] The point is that whatever one may think of Mariology — whether it is a profound comment on the meaning of womanhood or simply the male's specious tribute to womankind by putting one particular woman on such a high pedestal that women in the real world will be satisfied with a footstool (so Simone de Beauvoir, Mary Daley, et al.) — in any case it is impossible to use the Incarnation as a key to understanding the essence of femininity without weighting matters in favor of the masculine principle. Obviously, in the drama of salvation, the Son has the *primary* role, the mother the *secondary* role; he *operates*, she *cooperates*. In other words, the Eternal Masculine is on the divine side, the Eternal Feminine on the human side, of the universe.

It is difficult beyond measure for this writer to escape the suspicion that such an approach, in the last analysis, is simply an erudite statement of the man's understanding of himself as being like the Creator and of the woman as being like the creature. *He* is the image and glory of God; *she*, the glory of the man. If this is so, then in speaking of the Eternal Feminine we are really talking not about the way in which our male/female existence reflects ultimate reality, but rather about the way in which the male *conceives* this existence to reflect reality.[19]

Such an approach may indeed offer some authentic illustrations of the difference between masculine and feminine existence. No one can deny, for example, that a woman rules as a woman, not as a man; as a queen, and not as a king. But this is simply to recognize that because we are created men or women, all human activity reflects a qualitative distinction which is sexual in nature. But in my opinion, such an observation offers

18. It is doubtful, however, that one could reject the concept of the Eternal Feminine and accept Marian dogma, since the development of Marian dogma reflects the fundamental attitude toward woman expressed in the concept of the Eternal Feminine.

19. This problem can hardly be overcome by shifting from the dogma of the Incarnation to that of the Trinity. While the fellowship of the Father, the Son, and the Spirit may be reflected in our male/female fellowship at the human level (Barth's *analogia relationis*), such trinitarian terms as "generation" and "spiration" are too obscure to bear the theological freight of the distinction between the Eternal Masculine and the Eternal Feminine.

no clue to the ultimate meaning of that distinction. It may well be that we shall never know what that distinction ultimately means. But this much, at least, seems clear: we will understand the difference — what it means to be created as man *or* woman — only as we learn to live as man *and* woman in a true partnership of life.

Bibliography

Sources Contributing to the Discussion in a Significant Way

Andelin, Helen B., *Fascinating Womanhood*. Santa Barbara: Pacific Press, 1971.

Aquinas, Thomas, *Summa Theologica*. New York: Benziger Brothers, 1947.

Bailey, D. S., *Sexual Relation in Christian Thought*. New York: Harper & Bros., 1959.

Baltensweiler, Heinrich, *Die Ehe im Neuen Testament*. Zurich: Zwingli Verlag, 1967.

Barth, Karl, *Kirchliche Dogmatik*, III/1; III/2; III/4. Zollikon-Zurich: Evangelischer Verlag, 1945, 1948, 1951. [*Church Dogmatics*, III/1. Tr. J. W. Edwards, O. Bussey, and Harold Knight. Edinburgh: T. & T. Clark, 1958. III/2. Tr. Harold Knight, G. W. Bromiley, J. K. S. Reid, and R. H. Fuller. Edinburgh: T. & T. Clark, 1960. III/4. Tr. A. T. Mackay, T. H. L. Parker, Harold Knight, Henry A. Kennedy, and John Marks. Edinburgh: T. & T. Clark, 1961.]

de Beauvoir, Simone, *The Second Sex*. New York: Alfred A. Knopf, Inc., 1952.

Berdyaev, Nicholas, *The Destiny of Man*. London: Geoffrey Bles, 1954.

Berkouwer, G. C., *Man: the Image of God*. Grand Rapids: Eerdmans Publishing Co., 1962.

Bliss, Kathleen, *The Service and Status of Women in the Churches*. London: S.C.M. Press, 1952.

Brunner, Emil, *Das Gebot und die Ordnungen*. Tübingen: J.C.B. Mohr (Paul Siebeck), 1933.

Brunner, Emil, *Dogmatik*, II. Zurich: Zwingli Verlag, 1950 [*Dogmatics*, II. Tr. Olive Wyon. London: Lutterworth, 1952.]

Brunner, Emil, *Der Mensch im Widerspruch*. Zurich: Zwingli Verlag, 1937. [*Man in Revolt*. Tr. Olive Wyon. New York: Scribner, 1939.]

Calvin, John, *Commentaries*. Grand Rapids: Wm. B. Eerdmans Publishing Co., 1964.

Calvin, John, *Institutes of the Christian Religion*. Philadelphia: Presbyterian Board of Christian Education, 1936.

Eichrodt, Walther, *Theologie des Alten Testaments*. Leipzig: Heinrichs Verlag, 1939. [*Theology of the Old Testament*. Philadelphia: Westminster Press, 1961.]

von le Fort, Gertrude, *The Eternal Woman*. Milwaukee: Bruce Publishing Company, 1962.

Friedan, Betty, *The Feminine Mystique*. New York: W. W. Norton & Co., 1963.

Galling, Kurt, et al., ed., Die Religion in Geschichte und Gegenwart. Tübingen: J.C.B. Mohr (Paul Siebeck), 3 Auflage, 1958.

Grosheide, F. W., Commentary on the First Epistle to the Corinthians (The New International Commentary on the New Testament). Grand Rapids: Eerdmans Publishing Co., 1953.

Hutchins, Robert M., ed., Great Books of the Western World, Encyclopedia Britannica, Chicago, 1957.

Jeremias, Joachim, Jerusalem in the Time of Jesus. Philadelphia: Fortress Press, 1969.

von Kirchbaum, Charlotte, Die Wirkliche Frau. Zurich: Evangelischer Verlag, 1949.

Kittel, Gerhard, ed., Theological Dictionary of the New Testament. Grand Rapids: Wm. B. Eerdmans Publishing Co., 1964ff.

Leipoldt, J., Die Frau in der antiken Welt und im Urchristentum. Gütersloher Verlagshaus (Gerd Mohn), 1962.

Leon-Dufour, Xavier, ed., Vocabulaire du Theologie Biblique. Paris: Les Editions du Cerf, 1962.

Moll, Willi, Die Dreifach Antwort der Liebe. Graz: Verlag Styria, 1964. Father and Fatherhood. Notre Dame: Fides Pub., 1966.

Moll, Willi, The Christian Image of Women. Notre Dame: Fides Pub., 1967.

Niebuhr, Reinhold, The Nature and Destiny of Man. New York: Charles Scribner's Sons, 1941.

Phipps, William E., Was Jesus Married? New York: Harper and Row, 1970.

Plass, Ewald M., What Luther Says. St. Louis: Concordia Publishing House, 1959.

Sayers, Dorothy, Are Women Human? Grand Rapids: Wm. B. Eerdmans Publishing Co., 1971.

Schaff, Philip, History of the Christian Church. 8 vols. Grand Rapids: Wm. B. Eerdmans Publishing Co., 1955.

Stendahl, Krister, The Bible and the Role of Women. Philadelphia: Fortress Press, 1966.

Thomas, W. Derek, "The Place of Women in the Church at Philippi," The Expository Times, Jan. 1972, vol. 84, no. 4.

Thielicke, Helmut, Theologische Ethik. 3 vols. Tübingen: J.C.B. Mohr (Paul Siebeck), 1958.

Trible, Phyllis, "Depatriarchalizing in Biblical Interpretation," Journal of the American Academy of Religion, vol. 41, March 1973.

White, Andrew Dickson, The History of the Warfare of Science with Theology in Christendom. New York: D. Appleton & Co., 1955, vol. II.

Index of Subjects

Index of Names

Index of Scripture References

CPSIA information can be obtained
at www.ICGtesting.com
Printed in the USA
FSHW011953191020
75030FS